HOW
GET A
GRIP

D0130242

HOW TO GET A GRIP

**Forget namby-pamby,
wishy-washy, self-help drivel.
This is the book you need**

MATTHEW KIMBERLEY

Published by

an imprint of John Blake Publishing Ltd,
3 Bramber Court, 2 Bramber Road,
London W14 9PB, England

www.johnblakepublishing.co.uk

First published in paperback in 2011

ISBN: 9781843583288

All rights reserved. No part of this publication may be reproduced,
stored in a retrieval system, or in any form or by any means, without
the prior permission in writing of the publisher, nor be otherwise
circulated in any form of binding or cover other than that in which
it is published and without a similar condition including this condition
being imposed on the subsequent publisher.

British Library Cataloguing-in-Publication Data:

A catalogue record for this book is available from the British Library.

Design by www.envydesign.co.uk

Printed in Great Britain by CPI Bookmarque, Croydon, CR0 4TD

3 5 7 9 10 8 6 4 2

© Text copyright Matthew Kimberley

Papers used by John Blake Publishing are natural, recyclable products made from
wood grown in sustainable forests. The manufacturing processes conform to the
environmental regulations of the country of origin.

Matthew Kimberley lives in Malta and is an enforcer of common-sense.
He helps people get unstuck, both in life and in business. Find out
more at www.matthewkimberley.com

għal Sam
m'għandekx idea kemm inħobbok

CONTENTS

CONTENTS

CONTENTS

ACKNOWLEDGEMENTS

THANKS TO CLARE Christian, who picked me out of the slightly fetid corner of the internet I was dwelling in and is ultimately responsible for all of this. Equal thanks go to Lewis Crofts for showing me that the process of writing a book is a lot easier if you don't drink on school nights. Naomi Dunford has been a source of bullshit-free motivation and every semi-colon in this book is dedicated to her. John Hargreaves taught me how to read and write and made it all rather exciting. A lover of fine literature, he will find little merit in the pages that follow. Sonia Simone, Chris Brogan, Darren Rowse and Brian Clark have provided me with a sounding board and source of inspiration in their Third Tribe, which continues to be singularly distracting and rather a lot of fun. Michael Port, unbeknown to him, encouraged me to Think Big and morph the short, snappy, blog postings – which I'm sure he has neither read nor would approve of – into something which is longer, more informative and probably rather rambling. Will Gilroy is responsible for the profanity. Erica Swanson wrote the first draft of the chapter about keeping your house in order and is uniquely positioned to help you with the same. The mysterious Sasha and GirlPie have been supporters for reasons beyond my ken and I am grateful for their support and encouragement. Nina Lamparski got me writing again, before disappearing to the other side of the world to do useful stuff for people who need her help. Pamela Slim paid me a surprise compliment that provided me with the mind fuel to finish. Caroline Smailes gave some very wise advice at exactly the right time. Zoe McCarthy offered help and sagacity. Emma Beddington asked me to shout at her. Jonathan Fields suggested I go for a walk to clear my head. Dirk De Bruin sent me cash to buy coffees. I have stolen the word 'destuckifier' from the rather wonderful Havi Brooks. Imke Andert let me use her house and drink her coffee. The team at AdLib and John Blake were supporters and encouragers and sources of expertise. Very special thanks go to all the brilliantly clever and dashingly attractive readers of the blog.

And the biggest thanks of all goes to Gayle for putting up with me.

You're kind of cool. x

PREFACE

May all your choices in life be as wise as the choice you made to buy this book.

SOMETIMES IN LIFE, things get a bit shit. Some get it worse than others, but, whoever you are and whatever you do, you can't avoid it.

It's how you deal with the shit that sets you apart and, while you may think you lack the resources to turn things around and make it all a little less shit, you don't.

You have everything you need and you know all you need to know. In fact, you don't even need this book.

This book is simply a summary of everything you once knew but have since forgotten. And that's why you should read every word in this short but brilliant piece of literature.

You've probably read *a lot* of self-help stuff before (if you haven't – don't worry – you won't need to once you've finished this). Some of it has worked to some degree, for a brief moment of your life, but most of it hasn't worked at all.

None of the books you've picked up has made you more attractive to the opposite sex, a better conversationalist or a record-breaking Swedish javelin thrower. All they've done is given you a temporary morale boost before slinging you back into your grim state of under-washed underwear, over-stretched resources and perpetual dissatisfaction.

Books that claim to improve your life have been around for decades. They are designed to appeal to your insecurities, those scratchy and persistent voices that tell you that you aren't good enough, that you aren't rich enough, thin enough, strong enough or confident enough.

Admittedly, a lot of this earlier literature was good. A lot of the stuff that was written 80 or 90 years ago is still tight and true. Stuff like: treat people well and you'll find them more inclined to lend you their lawnmower. Stuff like: if you want to accumulate wealth, you've got to save more than you spend and not get three extra credit cards to finance your addiction to high-heels and Cosmopolitans.

But over the last few decades, something strange has happened to self-help literature: something inexplicable; something sinister.

If you're reading this in a bookshop, firstly, buy it already and take it home. But, on your way out, have a quick glimpse at the other books on the shelf. There are a few ethereal concepts up there, aren't there?

I'll bet you can find a tome that helps you *identify your angels*, without whom, it will claim, you're certainly fucked and destined to live in a polystyrene slum, snacking on cheesy biscuits and drinking Lambrini through a straw.

There'll be another book that helps you lose weight by changing your speech patterns. Look for the one called *Trim Six Inches Off Your Flabby Thighs With Neuro Linguistic Programming*.

And a third called *Set Your Child On The Route To A Fulfilling Career In The Medical Profession By Reading Him Bedtime Stories In Swahili*.

Angels are now involved in, no, *critical* to your general wellbeing, it appears. You ignore the power of crystals and chakras and positive manifestation and tribal incantations and other assorted witchcraftery at your peril. There are Secrets, we are told, that only the enlightened know, but are happy to share with you for £10.99. These are the kinds of secrets, presumably, that nobody's telling those cursed Somali kids living out their bad karma in a backwater of Mogadishu. It seems that nothing is easy to explain any more. You need to be finely attuned to your inner woo-woo or you're wasting your time.

Which is patently bollocks.

You already know everything you need to know about life. There's a whole load you really don't need to bother with and the answers to the really important questions you already have.

They're just buried deep in your subconscious under the answers to questions about whether you remembered to defrost the veal nuggets for dinner and if you remembered to validate your parking permit.

When you're honest with yourself, you'll realise that you already know how to be richer, thinner, a better lover, less brash, better company, less hirsute, more caring and less sensitive. You know what it is you need to do to get more sex, or hang out more with your kids, or eat more healthily.

You've wasted time on searching for 'the meaning of life'.

There is no meaning. It is what it is. *IL HAVE THAT ?*

But you knew that as well, didn't you?

That said, some things clearly have *more* meaning than others. Some stuff is more important.

What's important to you is *up to you* to determine. You already have a *very* good idea of what's important and what isn't. You understand that the key to really enjoying life is to take it less seriously and stop beating yourself up. That's what this book is about: defining the important shit, letting go of the less important shit, and taking your life – and yourself – a whole lot less seriously.

Because, once you've done that, you'll find that it's easier to be happy. And that's what you want, isn't it? You want to be ecstatic. You want to wake up each morning *on the verge of an orgasm* because you just know that your day is going to be filled with awesome and cupcakes and free beer.

And some days won't be awesome. And that's how it is. But, once you've read this book and you find yourself staring down a shitty day, you won't shake with needless anxiety or get an attack of the mind-cramps or take out your frustration on the cat, because this book will give you Advanced Ninja Skills in dealing with bad days. And these bad days come around despite your most valiant efforts.

So don't make your quest for happiness any tougher than it is. You *can* wake up with a mid-to-post-coital smile on your face, but you've managed to convince yourself that you can't do it alone.

With the interference of the self-help industry, you've come to believe that the game of living is a lot more difficult than it actually is. You're now entirely convinced that just about anything is insurmountable without some kind of intervention from a system or a seminar or an expert or a book or a workshop or a religion.

This book *is* an intervention and it's the last one that you'll ever need. It was easy to write, because it's a plain old vanilla rehashing of common sense, common knowledge and absolute truths, packaged up cunningly as a self-help guide.

It's the most important book you'll ever read. Buy three copies.

Nothing in these pages will surprise you, but a lot may delight you and even more will have you nodding your head in recognition and saying, 'Yes, I already know that.'

Let me repeat: you already know that.

But you've forgotten because of the noise.

The noise comes from everywhere: TV, magazines and well-meaning family members, church leaders, newspaper columnists, clothes designers and life coaches. They've all got advice for you. You've sought it out actively in the past and it's confused you.

In your rush to understand why some of you are fat losers and some of you toned and athletic millionaires with numbered bank accounts in exotic locations, you've stopped listening to yourself and started listening to the experts. YOU ALREADY KNOW THE ANSWERS, now stop looking for validation.

- You're fat because of a calorie in/calorie out imbalance.
- You're not saving money because you're spending more than you earn.
- You're shit at tennis because you spend more time at the pub than you do at tennis lessons.

Unfortunately, these quick and easy explanations have become displaced by suggestions far more complicated.

It's time for honesty.

No more bullshit.

You KNOW what's important. You KNOW how to do stuff, you've just forgotten.

If anybody – really anybody at all – were asked to make a list of the stuff they thought was truly crucial to a rewarding, comfortable existence, the REALLY IMPORTANT STUFF, then, in no particular order, the list would read like this:

Health

Happiness

That's it. A few jokers would mention wealth or the accumulation of stuff that compensates for a tiny dick, but they'd be wrong. Those would be extra.

More cash is nice to have, for sure (and being poor never made anybody happy – except perhaps Gandhi and Mother Teresa). But it's easy to be poor and happy, and poor and happy *feels* good. Rich and happy feels pretty damn fine as well. But rich and miserable? That sucks.

YOU KNOW THIS, remember.

Yet, despite being endowed with this eternal knowledge, you keep fucking it up. You kill yourself by putting in the extra hours for your boss, which causes you to miss your kids' school plays. You fatten your already plump arse with a two-hour commute. You invest time and money in the TV instead of your relationships, and you still eat saturated fats by the bucket-load, even though you know they will put you 10 feet under in a reinforced coffin.

This book is a gentle exhortation to remember what you know and why it's important.

So well done for deciding it's time to get a grip. You're halfway there.

HOW TO USE THIS BOOK

IT'S A BOOK, dumb-ass. It's not for using, it's for reading, so read this[1].

You are responsible for yourself and you must start with approaching this powerful life-manual with the responsibility it merits. Here's how to make this book into a WOWSERS project that is guaranteed to turn you into a demi-god:

You can do what most people will do – skim the headlines, perhaps read half a chapter in bed before falling asleep and dribbling over it – and then stick it on a bookshelf or in a cupboard somewhere and forget about it. If you're posh, you might leave it on the banquette at your poodle's massage therapist.

---

[1] As a bonus, there will be occasional extra reading material available in the footnotes for no extra charge.

Then, in a few weeks or months or years, you'll say to yourself, 'Gosh, I think it's about time I bought myself a book on personal development, because I've still got issues.'

So you'll buy another book. If I'm lucky, it will be this one again and I'll be halfway to buying myself another cappuccino with the royalty cheque.

If it's not this one, it will be another one. Perhaps one called *What Polyphasic Sleepers Can Learn From The Dog Whisperer* or *You're Only As Great As The Good That The Spirit Of Your Dead Grandmother Manifests*[2].

Then you'll read that, regret buying it, and stick it on a bookshelf somewhere.

Repeat *ad infinitum*.

By way of illustration, I have a collection of *Teach Yourself* books on various foreign languages. *Teach Yourself Japanese, Bulgarian, Romanian and Spanish.*

Can I speak any of them?

Not a word.

That's because I do what most people do. I decide I'm going to learn a language, and think that by buying the book, reading it once and not doing any of the exercises or implementing any of the suggestions I will become fluent or at

---

[2] Not a word of a lie: I have just received an email inviting me to 'receive the vibrational change to the frequency of the Ascended Masters where you can channel the Rays for yourself – a modality that is not "learned but transferred"'.

least capable enough to talk my way out of arrest for offending public decency.

Of course, it doesn't work. It never does[3].

You need to do more than that. You need to do what *effective* and *efficient* folk do, and turn your reading of this book into an escape route from the tedium of nonsense.

The book is split up into sections and each one contains a number of lessons, perfect for reading on the toilet. So do just that. Read this book on the john. Sitting down for 600 words won't aggravate your haemorrhoids. Vindaloo, fizzy lager and a neurotic boss will aggravate your haemorrhoids.

Read a lesson a day. It won't take you more than 10 minutes. If you don't have 10 minutes, you need this book more than you know. Each lesson presents a brilliant idea. Some lessons include suggestions that you can implement immediately.

If you do so, your life will improve.

In fact, by implementing my idiot-proof suggestions, you'll morph, overnight, from being a friendless, wimpy and subservient doormat, perpetually vexed by the inequities and bum-deals life throws at you, to being a fucking SUPER-

---

[3] Important disclaimer: *do as I say, not as I do.* If you feel that makes me hypocritical, so be it. I'm happy to field your criticisms because you are wrong. If you find yourself telling your kids, 'Don't be nasty to each other' and then, a couple of hours later, pass a bitchy comment about the size of some dude's wife, it doesn't make you a hypocrite or a bad parent. It makes you human.

HERO, turning down offers of back-rubs and free margaritas all day long[4].

If you don't carry out my suggestions and you find that you're still wallowing, friendless and cold, in the same muddy rut as you were before you read this book, don't come running it to me.

It's not my fault. The outcome is up to you.

[4] Second important disclaimer: results not typical. The mentioned outcomes are based on the experiences of a few, exceptional individuals and the author and publishers make no warranty that you will experience similar results.

PART ONE

SORT YOURSELF OUT

YOU ONLY NEED to do three things to get a grip. These are the Golden Rules of Getting a Grip.

Firstly, you need to take responsibility for yourself. That means giving up on waiting for permission or instructions or scapegoats.

Secondly, you need to take yourself less seriously. When you take *yourself* less seriously, you'll take *life* less seriously. Life is not a competition, it's a game. There are no winners or losers. We all end up dead.

Thirdly, you need to get good at getting stuff done. Nothing specific, just stuff. You need to get good at getting stuff done *not* so that you can cram even more into your day, but so that the stuff that is filling your day isn't a chore.

There are other bits and pieces that can help you to get a grip, including, importantly, dealing with the other cretins that

1

we're forced to share the planet with. The right attitude to other people and how to interact with them will accelerate you on the journey to grip-dom, as will the right attitude to work and money.

But if you take only three lessons away from reading this book, let it be The Golden Rules:

Take responsibility for yourself

Take yourself less seriously and

Get stuff done.

You also need to be clear about what's important. Some things matter a lot. A lot of things don't matter at all. At the moment, you spend too much time worrying about the little stuff and that affects your ability to analyse the big stuff properly.

If you find yourself worrying about stupid stuff, you need to stop NOW.

Examples of stupid stuff:

- Whether your socks match
- How much to tip the server
- What people you don't like think of you
- That you missed the bin-collection day
- That you're about two pounds overweight
- Timekeeping

Focus on the BIG stuff:

- Your health
- Your family
- Your relationships

WHY?

Because sweating the small stuff takes up time and emotional energy, both of which are a finite resource.

In this chapter, you're going to work on your foundation. There's an illustrative parable, there are the notes and then there are the seven building blocks you need to lay down in order to get a grip.

The building blocks create the foundation. You build on the foundation to become a ROCK STAR.

Because, after all, it's very easy for me to tell you to take responsibility for yourself, but if you're lacking the confidence (Building Block # 3), or waiting for permission (Building Block # 2), or wimping and moaning and pissing your pants (Building Block # 7), then taking responsibility for yourself is going to become a Sisyphean[5] task.

So tackle this in small increments and soldier on, soldier. Soldier on.

[5] Very difficult.

AN ILLUSTRATIVE
INTRODUCTORY PARABLE

THERE WAS A LITTLE dude called Benjamin (not his real name: it's a made-up story).

Benjamin wasn't one of life's winners, not in the classic sense of the word. He wasn't born with a silver spoon in his mouth. The poor little sod wasn't even born with a wooden one. He was, however, born with a hole in his heart and a speech impediment that robbed him of the ability to pronounce the letters 'b', 'j' and 'm'.

Poor little fucker.

After a difficult infancy marked with dysentery and a bout of polio that left him lame in his left leg, his mother gave him to a man named Otis in exchange for a new mobile phone, a packet of cigarettes and twenty quid's worth of scratch cards.

Otis was not a good man. He was not a good man at all. He put Benjamin (or 'Enanin' as he had come to be known) immediately to work in a hot, pokey garment factory. Benjamin's job was to stick designer labels on to knocked-off handbags that would be sold to the ladies who lived on the hill.

Benjamin worked close to 18 hours a day, stopping for five minutes every six hours for a meal of leftover slops and a dirty glass of water. Benjamin was not paid for his labour and would sleep for five fitful hours under his workbench every night, the smell of glue and hot leather pervading his nostrils.

Three days after Benjamin's 12th birthday, Otis employed a cleaning lady called Gladys. Gladys's shift started at 10 o'clock every evening, just as Benjamin was finishing his own work. Her job was to scrub the work surfaces with industrial alcohol, collect the scraps of leather and cloth that had accumulated on the floor and hose down the entire shop-floor, taking special care to not disturb the sleeping workers who had taken to kipping on their desks to avoid getting wet.

Benjamin and Gladys struck up a friendship of sorts and within a few weeks she had started to bring him gifts. These gifts were always the same: she brought him marbles. She would bring glass marbles and clay marbles, big marbles and small marbles. She would quietly explain the different names of these marbles and Benjamin came to know these names himself. He learned about oilies and chinas, peewees and King Kongs, cats-eyes, tigers and Indians. Soon he was telling Gladys the names of the marbles and even inventing some new names for the marbles that neither of them could recognise. He arranged them by size and by colour and hid them under the floorboards in the latrines, where he knew Otis would never look.

Benjamin lived for these marbles. He delighted in looking at them, and came to amass quite a collection of these pieces of coloured glass. By his 16th birthday, he had at least two hundred different marbles of different sizes and different hues. He had never been happier and would sing himself to sleep every night.

Then he got pneumonia and died.

Gladys paid for his tombstone. It reads:

'Here lies Benjamin. The happiest little bugger who ever walked the earth.'

At the same time, in the same fictitious village, while Benjamin was toiling in the factory, there lived in a house on a hill a lady named Sophia. Sophia was a true lady. She had long painted nails and everything.

She was healthy, beautiful and tall. Her time at finishing school had furnished her with elegant elocution, and Daddy, who was very much still alive, made sure that her allowance of several thousand pounds was paid promptly each month. She had six servants and manicured lawns. Her day was largely taken up with long lunches and massage.

Alas, Sophia was permanently angry because Jeannine, that *bitch*, had told her that her new handbag was *so* last season.

Sophia never forgave Jeannine. She never left the house again and died the night before her 28th birthday from too much gin and Xanax.

Nobody missed her, not really.

THE MORAL AND
THE LESSON

BENJAMIN WAS HAPPY with his lot. Sophia wasn't happy, despite having everything she could have needed by way of material comfort.

The moral of the story is to appreciate what you've got. That is the ONLY way to be happy and fulfilled. Full stop.

If you can't learn to APPRECIATE, then you're striving for an unquantifiable, indefinable *something* that you'll never find. You're either happy with your lot, or you're not. Get a grip. Celebrate the good shit in your life.

The knack for appreciating what they've got is why poor people can be happy.

This is also why people who own planes and corporations and lion-skins are able to be permanently dissatisfied, striving incessantly for more. More isn't better. More *can* be great, but it's how you look at your 'more' that determines it.

I'm not suggesting you begin each morning with positive incantations, power-breathing and sun salutations. I'm not suggesting you pin post-it notes to your mirror to remind you that you are wonderful, unique and in control of your destiny. I'm *certainly* not proposing that you convince yourself that you are capable of anything by listening repeatedly to self-hypnosis tapes.

Quite the opposite, actually.

What you need to do is remind yourself that WHAT YOU'VE GOT IS OK.

And even more than that: HALF OF WHAT YOU'VE GOT WOULD BE OK.

SO LOWER YOUR EXPECTATIONS.

In lowering your expectations and being happier with less, you can drastically improve your satisfaction levels.

Are you a Benjamin or a Sophia? A grateful, cheeky tike with a love for life and appreciation of the simpler things, or a spoiled, manipulative bitch who can't be satisfied no matter what?

Ask yourself how good you've got it.

Now ask yourself again.

Change your perspective, do a life-inventory, and you'll find that you've got no reason to complain[6].

AND LEARN WHEN TO STOP.

---

[6] If you're still not sure about this, the mere fact that you've spent money on a self-help book would indicate that perhaps you've got it better than you might think.

More isn't always best. The world would be top-heavy if all the world's bakers went on to be Michelin-starred chefs, or all the world's cleaners went on to become psychotherapists.

Advancement and progress are what keeps civilisation civilised. But they're also what gave us nuclear weapons and daytime TV.

You need to set your own parameters and stop living up to the expectations handed down to you by others.

In fact, if you find that you're getting a bit stressed living up to other people's expectations, then this piece of advice will help: STOP.

Just stop it dead.

Yes, ambition is perfectly healthy as long as it's YOUR ambition.

* * *

You: *'EUREKA! I know exactly what I want to do! I want to be a nurse and look after sick people!'*

Well-meaning relative: *'Brilliant! I can only encourage you. And what's great about that is that being a nurse is only one step away from being a doctor! And once you've qualified as a doctor you can specialise in surgery and then plastic surgery. Once you've got a few years of experience and a bit of a name for yourself, you can open your own practice, maybe in Beverly Hills, and then, with two decades of heavy self-promotion and long hours you can get your own TV show, write a best-selling book and employ a dozen staff and by the age of 55 you'll be earning millions and you'll never have to work again.'*

You: *'But I want to be a nurse...'*

* * *

Enough is enough!

And why is 'enough is enough' something we only ever say about bad shit? Why do we only say it when Bernadette and her brother Bertrand keep pulling each other's hair in the back seat of the car, or your mother-in-law passes *another* snide remark about your curtains and your hairdo and your weight?

Why do we only say ENOUGH IS ENOUGH when bad things are getting on top of us?

Say it when shit is good as well. *'Gosh – this mung-bean stir-fry is awesome, but I've had enough.'* Or *'Gosh – I think that's more than enough promotions for this year, I'm off on holiday before they make me CEO.'* Or *'Gosh, I don't really know what to do with another car. I'll stick with the one I've got, thanks.'*

Knowing how to say 'I have enough' is the key to satisfaction. I'm not talking about being self-satisfied, I'm talking about CONTENTMENT, that elusive non-tangible that we pay yogis thousands of our sweat-soaked pounds for.

If you don't know when to stop, you'll end up over-shooting your destination and falling off the edge of the world into a pit of fiery fish soup.

So take a minute to define for yourself what ENOUGH looks like. Now stick to it.

The more you have, the more you want. The more you want, the fatter you will become. The fatter you become, the more miserable you will be.

Remember:

- Be happy with what you've got
- Lower your expectations
- Know when enough is enough

BUILDING BLOCK #1:
ASSUME RESPONSIBILITY

ANY IMPETUS TO get off your fat arse and do something that YOU have deemed useful and worthwhile has to come *from you*.

Whose fault is it that you can't get out of bed without a battle and you prefer to spend your mornings lying prone, sipping milky coffee, smoking Lambert & Butler and dropping crisp crumbs all over your polyester sheets? Whose fault is it that you're not getting dressed and talking to interesting people about the burning issues of the day?

Whose fault is it that your kitchen is a health hazard? Who left congealed Dairylea triangles in the fridge on top of what was once a packet of economy bacon? Whose fault is it that you didn't go on holiday this year but instead spent your paltry bonus on 15 extra TV channels and a turquoise shell-suit? Who's to blame that you don't make the effort to have sex, but expend plenty of effort on complaining that you're not getting enough?

It's YOUR fault.

YOU are responsible for yourself. YOU are responsible for your health. YOU are responsible for the state of your kitchen and size of your waist and the amount of oral sex you can command. YOU are responsible for your wellbeing and happiness and productivity and haircut and job prospects and bank balance and wardrobe.

Sure, shit happens. It happens to you and it happens to everybody. Spanners get thrown, gremlins get loose and mighty cans of whoop-ass get opened when you're not expecting it.

Some have it worse than others. Some of us were born in the arse-end of the country to a family of inbred petty criminals with facial tattoos and Neolithic attitudes to women and literacy. Some of us lost brothers and sisters in horrific accidents and some of us got mightily fucked over by employers, muggers, school bullies and the taxman. Some of us were hit by cars, maimed by itinerant psychopaths, neglected by casually cruel parents and bankrupted by con-artists with flash watches, camel-hair coats and appealing patter. Some of us were young and dumb enough to get tribal piercings that gave us blood infections from which we've never truly recovered.

Some of this we can get over. Facial tattoos can be removed. Physiotherapy can strengthen withered limbs. But some stuff is tougher to shift. How do we cope with the stuff that can't be removed with an ointment or a scan or a spot of non-invasive surgery? What about the stuff like the heartache and the suffering and emotional scars and the grief and the psychological trauma that all of us, to some degree, have to carry through life?

That's simple. You either learn to live with it, or you don't.

What's the difference between those who come through, breathing and laughing and wearing Rolexes on the other side of a terrible time, and those who can't get up off their backsides and brush themselves off?

Why do some of us spring back and ATTACK and resolve and fight and grapple our way out of misery and muck and the rest of us wallow in never-ending concentric circles of self-pity, self-loathing and resignation?

The difference is this:

Some people TAKE RESPONSIBILITY.

Some people blame the world for every woe that befalls them, and then carry on blaming the world for each subsequent fuck-up, omission and spectacular failure that ensues. These people are grateful to not shoulder any responsibility. These people have washed their hands of life.

They've got their scapegoat and they're sticking with it. These are people who don't get stuff done.

These are people who say, 'Yes, I was going to go on holiday this year, but I have to work on a REALLY important project for Mega Bank plc. There'll be plenty of time for holidays when I retire.' These are the people who say, 'I won't ever be able to afford...' and 'I wish...' and 'in my dreams...'.

But then there are the others, the others who blame

circumstances beyond their control when it's appropriate and blame themselves when they're to blame.

When the manure falls unexpectedly from a great height, they take a shower and say, 'I'll show you, you bastards,' and move on.

These are the folk who say 'when' instead of 'if' and 'let's make it happen' instead of 'it's impossible'.

Which camp do you belong to?

You can't control the volume, quantity or colour of the shit that will get thrown at you from the minute you arrive in this world, incontinent and bawling, to the moment you leave, similarly afflicted.

You *can* control, however, whether you're going to clutch a shovel and get stuck into breaking out of the gargantuan piles of ordure, or whether you're going to don a snorkel and just about survive while the crap piles on in ever-increasing bucket-loads.

If you're already beating yourself up over every little thing; if you find that your already dubious standards of personal hygiene are slipping and you think it's OK to wash your hair every other week, and that showers are only for really dirty people and that tracksuits and football shirts are suitable casual-wear, then you need to start working on yourself.

If you're a slave to the vagaries of your employer and you do all you can to appease the fat halitosis-ridden bastard, then you need to start working on yourself.

If your best friends are jobless smack-heads and alcoholics and you're *still* wondering why you haven't had a birthday card for three years, then it's time to start working on yourself.

This book will help. This book will change your life, but you have to allow it to. Use it or don't. I don't care. Take some responsibility and watch things change rapidly for the better.

You can do it because you rock, even if you don't know it yet.

BUILDING BLOCK #2:
GIVE YOURSELF PERMISSION

QUIT WAITING ON being told stuff is OK. What are you, six?

That said, you had more balls when you were six, didn't you? You just went ahead and did shit even if you *knew* it wasn't allowed. When you were young, it was cute or cheeky or spirited.

Nowadays, rule-breakers are spoken about in whispers and not invited to garden parties and dragged through the courts. You can't bear the thought of that (*what would the neighbours say?*), so you cower in your suburban semi and wait to do what you're told.

This is no good. This is a problem that needs a solution.

And this is the solution:

Adopt the mindset of a six-year-old and become your own authority. Become the Emperor of You dot com. At the moment you're afraid because you don't see yourself as an authority. In fact, you have this sick idea of authority that has you placed firmly at the bottom of the people-pile.

The people-pile is your imaginary hierarchy of humans that has you at the bottom, waiting on the scraps and opportunities that are doled out to you by the folk at the top, the folk with titles and gold chains who *authorise* stuff.

But you're not at the bottom of the people-pile, you're at the top. Get back on your horse.

After all, what are authority figures? They're people, flawed and fickle and saggy examples of mankind with people to answer the phone for them. Big deal, they still take difficult dumps the morning after a big dinner.

You're the Queen of Sheba. Now get on with whatever it is you want to get on with.

Get on with *anything*. If it's been six months since you last inflicted your rendition of 'I Will Survive' on the world, give yourself permission to have a girls' night out. Get smashed and pull a sickie.

The world will not stop functioning.

You're an old dude? Get a skateboard. Seriously: give yourself permission to skateboard. So what if you've got a paunch? You'll look like a dick? Good! Give yourself permission to look like a dick.

Everything you do has a consequence, for sure, and maybe that's what's been holding you back from the abseiling or extra-marital affair or corporate power-grab or Arctic trek, but, if you don't try, you won't find out what the consequences are.

So what do you want to do? You want to say to your wife, '*Listen, I'm going out with the boys*'? Say it.

You want to tell your husband, '*I don't feel like cooking for you tonight*'? Don't say that. Say '*I'm* not *cooking for you tonight*.'

Ask yourself for permission. Then say yes.

You'll be one step closer to getting a grip.

BUILDING BLOCK #3:
BE CONFIDENT

IN ORDER TO become your own authority and dole out permission to yourself to get on with the good stuff life has to offer, you're going to have to believe you have that authority. You need to work on your confidence levels, sunshine.

Today, you're a wall-flower. You position yourself according to other folk and find yourself lacking. And so you lack self-confidence.

Loser.

Here's the thing, and you'll do well to stay with me and concentrate over the next couple of paragraphs, it gets a little tricky. If you're half intelligent[7], then you're going to be *just* a little bit judgemental.

---

[7] You are intelligent. In fact, as a purchaser and peruser of this book I'd say you fall into the upper 95th percentile of intelligent folk the world over.

You're a little bit judgemental because intelligent people like you have opinions. These opinions are mostly about other people.

Some of your opinions are favourable. Some of them are even gushing. There are some people out there who you would lie down over shitty puddles for, just so that they don't get their Manolo Blahniks soiled.

Some folk you hold in such high esteem that you would wipe your sweaty brow with their soiled briefs if you thought it would give them pleasure.

And then there are the other folk, other folk who aren't so brilliant. And worse: the other folk who are definitely lacking in the brilliant stakes but remain obstinately convinced of their own luminosity. These are people who talk too much or who chew too loudly or who wear tracksuits and trainers off the sports field.

Your opinion of them isn't so high. Sometimes you'd like to do them physical damage. Sometimes you cross the street to avoid them. And, just once, you seriously considered planting drugs in their living room and tipping off the police.

This is OK. You should celebrate this variety of opinion. You'd get cheek spasms from smiling if you thought everybody was great and you'd get arrested if everybody wound you up. We were born to polarise. If we all thought the same or held the same beliefs or ate the same brand of breakfast cereal, then we'd all be mightily fucked and living out a bland, pre-processed existence without any interesting disagreements after a three-martini lunch.

And other people think the same (not that you need external validation, but it's good to know you're not unique – who wants that?). That's to say, other people have differing opinions about the other people in their lives.

Therefore, working on the assumption that everybody's got an opinion about everybody else, and also working on the assumption that your intelligence levels are higher than everybody else's, there's no good reason for a lack of self-confidence.

I'll write that again:

There is no good reason for a lack of self-confidence.

Self-confidence isn't really a good way of describing the way you feel about yourself. It's a misnomer. At root, confidence in ourselves comes from other people's confidence in us. The more I tell you that you are brilliant, the more you will believe me. The more I tell you that you are slightly naff, the more you will believe me, even despite your best efforts, and the more naff you will feel.

It's more powerful when amplified through repetition. If enough people put you down enough times, then eventually their words will become redundant, because you'll be doing such a fine job of putting yourself down you won't need anyone else's input.

Or perhaps you're doing a good job of putting yourself down without the intervention of other people. Perhaps you think you know what others are thinking. You say, '*Since my stroke three years ago I'm half the man used to be. I might as well just curl up in a little ball and ignore the world, because the world is ignoring me.*'

22

But you'd be wrong. You don't know what others are thinking.

Your SELF-confidence is proportional to how you believe others see you.

If you're suffering from a lack of self-confidence, or low self-esteem, you need to remember the following: you haven't got a clue what other people are thinking. You reckon you're a mind-reading voodoo expert, but, actually, you're clueless. Stop making your place on earth relative to everybody else's.

1. What other people are thinking doesn't matter anyway, as you're smarter than 95 per cent of them.
2. Therefore, you can, with great justification, say a big 'fuck you' to everybody out there.

Remind yourself that you rock. And take it to extremes, as *the solution to a genuine lack of self-confidence is a temporary surfeit of the stuff.*

So tell the rest of the world that you rock. Shout it loud.

And, once you're playing the same game as the rest of the retards around you, you'll realise you can stop bluffing, because we're all a little screwed, and we're all a little self-conscious and we're all a little shy.

But some of us are better liars.

BUILDING BLOCK #4:
BE DECISIVE

A DECISION IS made when a confident person gives themselves permission to choose between two or more options.

That's why you're so fucking awful at taking decisions today. You're stuck on the confidence and the permission bit.

But now you're the Chief Executive Officer of You dot com, decision-making is starting to get easier.

Up until now, you've said:

'I like to leave things up to fate. If it's meant to be, it's meant to be!'

And you've been walked all over.

You pussy-foot around, umming and aaahing, humming and haawing and NOTHING gets done. You end up with a list of things you never did and regret not doing. You feel sorry for yourself. You end up shoeless and overweight with food caught in your beard.

Change your life, cowboy! BE A DECISION-MAKER!

HOW TO MAKE A DECISION

1. Limit your choices. Chunk down, eliminate, slice and discard options like an option-discarding ninja on an elimination spree. If you're faced with 16 great opportunities, chuck 13 of them out without even glancing. There'll be another day for those.

2. Make a decision. This is the 'take massive action' step and requires you to eliminate another option or two. Give yourself a time limit for this task. I suggest eight seconds for 'what to wear', one minute for 'how to mix the perfect martini',[8] five minutes for 'Caribbean or Pacific islands' and perhaps a little longer for identifying a surrogate mother.

3. Never look back – quit with the 'what-ifs'. Enough with the 'if-onlys'. Don't apologise and don't explain. Make another decision next week.

Being able to make a decision improves your life in untold ways. You will, for example, get more sex. Take this example.

You're out to dinner at Chez Antoinette. There are 18 pages on the menu and, although you don't understand everything, you pretend you do. The sexy guy from marketing has already chosen steak and fries. You don't know whether to go for the fritto misto, or the lapin à la kriek, the quails' eggs Benedict or the truffle omelette. The parmesan soufflé looks divine and you've heard great things

[8] You will never get this right. Let it go.

25

about the sea-bass casserole. You take a few minutes. You take a few minutes more to contemplate the enchiladas.

You take for-fucking-EVER and the hot guy from marketing has you down as a neurotic ingrate who's depriving him of his meat.

You go home alone to feed your cats and drink a solitary bottle of Blue Nun.

VERSUS

The hot guy from marketing says, 'I'll have steak and fries.'

You say, 'Me too.'

You don't go home for four days, and, when you do, you're saddle-sore.

This is what will ACTUALLY happen when you become more decisive.

Being able to make a decision is how you practically implement the 'responsibility' and 'permission' building blocks.

After all, you know the people you really admire, your role models, your gurus? Do they make firm, concrete, definite and rapid decisions?

Of course they do.

And now you do, too.

You rock.

BUILDING BLOCK #5:
STOP MAKING IT SO DIFFICULT

STOP MAKING SHIT so difficult! Seriously, dude, you're your own arch-nemesis when it comes to making really simple things mind-gnawingly difficult.

There's a world of practical difference between simple and easy. Simple is the idea you have and the execution of that idea is the bit that *should* be easy, but rarely is.

Almost everything you will have to deal with is simple (unless you're into advanced genetics or microeconomics). There is nothing that you want to do or achieve that is not simple. You want to take a trip to Bali? Simple – get on a flight. You want to go back to university? Simple – enrol.

Tons of stuff is simple. Tons of stuff is simple beyond simple.

To prove how simple just about anything is, write it down.

Try this for starters: '*Tomorrow morning I'm going to wake up at six, stretch my Achilles tendons for four-and-a-half minutes, perform 16 repetitions of pelvic-floor exercises, peel a mango, blitz some spinach and squeeze a lime for my breakfast smoothie before getting showered, dressed and shaved. I'll be in work at six-thirty.'*

There, simple, isn't it?

And yet why can't you translate simple into easy?

Come tomorrow morning, your alarm clock rings at five-to-six. But, rather than jump out of bed, grabbing the day by the balls and easing your tight ankles and loose bladder, you hit the snooze button and wake up in just enough time to avoid being late for another day at the steel mill.

Or another example: *'In December I'm going to take that once-in-a-lifetime trip to the Arctic Circle. I've been promising myself this trip for the last 43 years. I shall book it immediately.'*

And yet you don't. You don't book it immediately, because the minute you start to think about it, you come up with a thousand reasons why it's not the best time to do it. What if you're not physically up to it? We're in the middle of an economic crisis and you might not have any money. Great Auntie Vera and her leaky poodle have been talking about coming to visit for the last three Christmases: this might be the year she actually comes.

And what about if you actually do go ahead and book your trip and go and enjoy it? What will be left of your life? What will you have to look forward to?

After all, trips to the Arctic Circle are the reserve of *other people*, aren't they? The other people at the top of the people-pile, who aren't you. Other people who were put on earth to do that kind of stuff.

It's better if you don't go. That way you can always talk about how much you want to go. Agreed?

* * *

I was once watching daytime TV, the result of a particularly insistent hangover. There was some boiler-plate background-noise show on called *How Much Is The Crap Stuffed Down The Back Of Your Sofa Worth At Auction?*

Beryl was the lucky pleb who had the cameras into her bungalow that week. At the point in the programme where I tuned in, Beryl had just shifted some Victorian doilies for a hundred quid. The orange-mugged presenter asked her what she'd do with the money. 'Well, I'm not sure,' said Beryl.

'Come on,' said the presenter. 'How will you treat yourself? What do you like to do? What are your interests?'

'Well,' said Beryl, 'I've never actually *done* it, but there *is* something I've always wanted to do.'

'Excellent,' said the presenter, 'and what's that?'

'Well,' said Beryl again, 'I've always wanted to try line-dancing.'

Line-dancing.

The tumbleweed crashed audibly across the screen.

This poor, stupid woman, who had reached close to 60 years of age, had never been line-dancing. DESPITE HAVING ALWAYS WANTED TO![9]

Beryl, for God's sake! Treat yourself better! Make your life simpler!

But, as you know, there are a thousand reasons and excuses for not making simple easier.

In your case, it could have been your peers, your family or your interested others who are more concerned with reinforcing the status quo than encouraging you forward, because they're terrified you might leave them behind.

Beryl's husband had probably squashed her dreams years ago. '*Why would you want to make a tit of yourself doing daft shit like that?*' he probably asked her in between eating his sausage roll and scratching his balls.

Or more likely, the fault lay with Beryl, like the fault lies with you. You are the obstacle in your own way. What if, just for a minute, you pretended that you didn't have a choice? What if a simple idea NEEDED to be implemented?

- Simple: I'm going to run a mile in five minutes.
- Easy? No.
- VERSUS

[9] Line-dancing, for the lucky uninitiated, is dancing by numbers. The barriers to entry are remarkably low. You go to any parochial village hall any week of the year, pay about £2, and some guy in a cowboy hat tells you to step backwards and forwards in time to pre-recorded music. There is orange squash available for refreshment.

- Simple: I'm going to run a mile in five minutes to deliver my son's blood transfusion or he might die.
- Easy? Fuck yes.

You have the resources, but you only use them when you don't have a choice. You can change that. Eliminate the choice. Stop making life so bloody difficult. Take a simple idea, tell yourself it's easy and you'll be surprised how often it is.

BUILDING BLOCK #6:
ELIMINATE STRESS

STRESS KILLS. Stress is caused by anxiety. Anxiety is bad.

Anxiety is caused by your reactions to situations and events. If you believe that the outcome of any specific situation has the potential to do us harm, then you're already halfway fucked.

Before you know it, you're pulling your hair out, losing sleep and snapping at your husband[10].

Here's how to deal with anxiety:

Minimise the number of events and situations that cause you to poo your pants a little. Not by *avoiding* these situations but by redefining what actually *does* cause you real harm.

---

[10] Your husband (or wife) may very well be the cause of your stress. He (or she) may also be a convenient scapegoat. I'm working on the assumption that most arguments within the family aren't caused by any specific tension BETWEEN two people, but rather a rising tension in ONE of the two people that ends up involving both of them.

There's nothing more soul-destroying and mind-numbing than *unnecessary* anxiety.

Legitimate anxiety is anxiety for your own safety and for the safety of others. If you're teetering on the edge of a slippery cliff with nothing but a packet of wine-gums to break your fall, you may give yourself permission to experience legitimate anxiety. If you're skinny-dipping to celebrate your graduation and realise that you're five miles out to sea and too drunk to swim another five metres, you may experience legitimate anxiety.

But if your anxiety is caused by being afraid of *looking* stupid or amateur or unsophisticated, then your anxiety is anything but legitimate and a drain on your mental, intellectual and sexual capacities. You will not get laid if you are in a state of terror, and you will not be happy if you don't get laid.

Answer the following questions honestly. Have you ever:

- Experienced acute discomfort and bladder pain because you were too embarrassed to ask to use the toilet in a strange place?
- Been served an awful meal in an expensive restaurant that you're *supposed* to enjoy, and when asked by the waiter how it is, replied with something like, 'Oh, absolutely delicious, thanks,' for fear of causing offence?
- Avoided asking your boss for a raise because you're afraid he might say no?
- Failed to stand up to the crowd of braying haters when

they're kicking the little man when he's down, in case they mark you out as a bore?

If you answered yes to any of the above questions, don't worry. You're not alone. But you need to kill these little harbingers of stress as soon as they appear. Or they will kill you.

BUILDING BLOCK #7:
MAN THE FUCK UP

THE FINAL BUILDING block in your foundation is to Man The Fuck Up. That means quitting your bitching, bleating, moaning and whining.

Quit dribbling about how the world treats you badly or about how your girlfriend dumped you or your boyfriend ran off with your sister or about how you didn't get that pay rise or promotion or win that deal. You'll be surprised how little anybody cares.

Quit sniffling and making excuses and looking for a scapegoat when you know that you're to blame. You're soft. Toughen up.

Quit blaming others and start taking responsibility for yourself. In short… Man The Fuck Up. And do it quickly.

Here's why:

There is NOTHING less attractive than the misery of other people. Sure, we all get a little hard-on from charity and beneficence and playing the good Samaritan when it's needed. Some of us even make it our life's mission to help out those in need.

But do you really want to be *needy*? Or do you want to be a self-sufficient superstar that is renowned throughout the land for your bright and bullish '*life can be shit, but look how cool I am*' attitude?

In bitching all the time, you're presuming that other people actually give a shit. But NOBODY cares about your problems as much as you care about them. And NOBODY (with the exception of your mother, perhaps) cares about YOU as much as you care about YOU.

Dude, you don't even have a friend in Jesus.

And if you're not a guy, and you don't think the exhortation to 'Man The Fuck Up' applies to you, then I'll rephrase it.

Grow Up.

This is about being a grown-up. One with a spinal column and control of your tear ducts.

If you decide that you can't take care of yourself, then you'll find that others feel the same way about taking care of you.

You know that friend of yours, the one who's always moaning? The one about whom you say '*she can be hard work – I'm not answering the phone*'?

Yes?

That's you, that is.

The thing is, unmanly, un-grown-up friend of mine, is that, if you say, '*I'm a loser*', others will only say, '*No, you're not*' a few times before they start to agree with you.

Stop snivelling. Stop moaning. Do not complain. You can deal with your anger and your chronic deficiencies without laying them on the world.

Talking about your problems helps resolve them. Incessantly blathering on about the shit you're going through does the opposite.

Man the fuck up.

PART TWO

GETTING STUFF DONE

WELL DONE. You've got the building blocks to making life suck less in place. Your foundation is firm. You're more decisive, less sensitive and you feel equipped to do pretty much anything, like you're carrying a super-fucking-duper toolbox for life around with you.

Congratulations. It didn't take long. Now it's time to put that toolbox to use and start doing all the shit that you're equipped to do.

This chapter contains some seriously practical advice for getting real, concrete results. We're not talking in metaphors any more. There are no more parables. This is just plain advice.

This is advice on how to do the stuff you have to do. It's how to get stuff shifted so that you can concentrate on the important other stuff.

Later on in the book, there'll be some SERIOUSLY practical

no-mucking-about suggestions. Stuff like 'clean up your bathroom, you filthy layabout. The tiles aren't meant to be grey and if anybody drops by for an emergency shower they won't trust you to prepare food any more.' It's stuff like 'there shouldn't be cobwebs under the toaster' and 'how to talk to people you don't know without becoming breathless and blotchy'.

But, in order to actually EXECUTE the suggestions that follow later on, you've got to know how to get stuff done.

But you already know how to get stuff done, don't you? You're not an idiot, you're perfectly capable of following instructions, aren't you?

Or are you?

The big difference between knowing how to do something and actually doing something is:

ACTION.   DO IT!

Action is the art of doing stuff. It sounds like this:

BANG! WALLOP! KERPOW!

Action (also known as 'execution') is the differentiating factor between Warren Buffett and your delusional Uncle Rudolph who tells you, 'Never invest in the stock-market, son. Bricks and mortar is the ONLY way to make money.' That's the same Uncle Rudolph who was arrested last July with a rucksack full of stolen cat food and was evicted from his hovel three weeks later.

Action is the difference between 'screw it, let's do it' and 'fuck it, let's have a kebab'.

And at the moment you're a kebab-muncher. But don't worry! Help is at hand.

In order to become one of those people who stops talking about doing and starts doing the doing, all you need to do is read the next chapter. If, by the end of it, you don't feel you've got all the tools necessary to go out there and be the Chief Executioner of Action Now Inc, then read it again. After all, if something is worth saying, it's worth saying twice. After all, if something is worth saying, it's worth saying twice.

If, after two readings, you still don't think you're ready, then I'll buy you a kebab[11].

In short, there are three steps to reclaiming your time and becoming more productive. Those three steps are:

Do it List

1. Identify all the shit that you're meant to be doing.
2. Work out which of those things you're meant to be doing NOW, which can be done LATER, which can be done by other people and which you don't actually have to do at all. And
3. Get on with doing it. *Do it!*

This chapter will take you from being a slovenly apathetic

---

[11] I won't actually buy you a kebab. I'm too busy doing stuff to take time off for kebabs. If this upsets you, I'm sorry. If you're really, *really* gutted that you won't be getting a kebab, I suggest you go straight to the section on 'Health'.

wreck, unable to work out what you're meant to be doing, unable to start doing stuff, entirely incapable of finishing stuff and running perpetually late, into a time-management master, swanning around slightly tipsy like a louche aristocrat with perfect hair.

GETTING STUFF DONE LESSON 1:
PRIORITISE

YOUR INABILITY TO IMPLEMENT is starting to cause you grief. Your kitchen sink is overflowing, your clothes are spread variously around your rather grimy apartment, your gut is rapidly expanding because you're not cooking properly and you're not working out, and the light-bulb on the landing has needed replacing for the last nine weeks.

In short, you have trouble managing your time in order to get the things that really need doing done.

You need a system to PRIORITISE what's got to be done and what doesn't have to be done just yet.

You say: '*Uurgh, I've got like one million things to do and I can't even get started on the smallest one because I'm so, like, blinking distracted and as soon as I start on one thing another five turn up and even just waking up in the morning I DON'T KNOW WHERE TO START!*'

Sound familiar?

SORT IT OUT!

You're not going to get anything done if you spend your entire day talking about doing stuff. You're keeping this information in your head and INSISTING that your head is the best place for it.

But what does it look like inside your head? Neat, ordered, each memory, personality trait, task to remember all neatly compartmentalised and easily accessible?

Or is it a hopeless swirl of sticky grey matter, with the really important struggling with the mundane to get to the surface and the clear light of day?

My money's on the second.

Here's how you remedy it:

BRAIN DUMP:

Brain-dumping is messy list-writing. You need to evacuate your mind-bowels on to a SINGLE piece of paper, and don't throw that piece of paper out until you've replaced it with another one.

Instructions:

1. Take a large piece of paper and a big, fat-tipped felt-tipped pen.
2. Without thinking too hard, write down all the LITTLE STUFF that's in your head that needs to be done pretty soon. Urgent stuff, like 'overdue tax return', 'polish shoes for this afternoon's job interview', 'apply for Yemeni visa for holiday next week', 'return optimistically purchased running

shoes to sports shop before refund date expires', etc. Write EVERYTHING down. Don't filter, don't analyse and don't hold back. There's time for analysis and reordering later on.

3. Take five minutes and boil some ginger tea or do a jigsaw puzzle or squeeze a stress-ball to release the tension that's developed in your hand from writing with a pen for the first time since school.   1 - 3 - 5

4. Take your large piece of paper and pen and write down all the MEDIUM-SIZED stuff. This stuff is less time-sensitive. Stuff like 'catch up with Fiona and forgive her for wearing the same outfit to Janice and Leonard's wedding last August', 'join a synchronised swimming team', or 'go to the cinema for the first time in eight years'.

5. Take five minutes again and talk to your house plants. It encourages their growth. If you don't have house plants, don't beat yourself up. Botany's not for everybody.

6. Back to the pen and paper and one final massive dump of brain matter all over the page. This is a brain dump of the BIG STUFF. This stuff is your life plans. This stuff is the BIG PICTURE stuff. Equally important, but not going to be done overnight. 'Tour Addis Ababa in a London taxi', 'write a best-selling novel' or 'get married to a rich man with a country pile and a dodgy heart'.

7. Voila! And BANG! You now have a TO-DO LIST made up of LITTLE STUFF, MEDIUM-SIZED STUFF and BIG STUFF. AWESOME!

8. Now get another piece of paper and put them in order of size. You no longer have a to-do list, but a LIFE PLAN. Seriously, dude, it took, like, 15 minutes!

9. Start to do stuff. Start with the LITTLE STUFF. Do the first thing on the list. Then the second. Cross each thing off as you finish it and watch as you achieve a sense of unprecedented wellbeing at the PROGRESS you're making at being a Doing Stuff MBA.

ADVANCED BRAIN DUMPING TECHNIQUES

The problem with this is that you never get to the BIG STUFF. Implementing the BIG STUFF is where this previously simple task starts to get tricky.

Make yourself very comfortable and clear some space between your ears to understand this next bit.

The BIG STUFF on the list – career planning, gender reassignment – can be broken down in other, smaller lists. Apply the same brain-dumping techniques to the BIG STUFF and watch yourself get closer day by day to the end result.

An example:

Your preliminary brain-dump resulted in the words 'Get Married To An Elderly Rich Man'.

You have no idea where it came from, but you're not going to argue now that it's written down. It's a great idea, after all. But it's not so simple, eh?

(This next step can be scary, but stick with me and you'll be on your way to a house with a swimming pool and holidays in St Tropez.)

1. Get a second piece of paper and write 'How I Will Marry an Elderly Rich Man' at the top, or 'How I Will Fulfil My Lifetime Dream of Selling Popcorn to the Vatican' or whatever your BIG STUFF goal may be.
2. Repeat steps 1–9 above, only this time focus only on the steps needed to secure your ultimate goal of an avaricious marriage of convenience. For example, you might need to get your hair done to look less like a swamp monster and more like an 18-year-old nymphette or you might need to start hanging out in home county country clubs or get introductions from elderly wealthy friends to their single buddies.
3. Whatever steps you identify, apply the same execution techniques as with your initial list. You'll have more lists, for sure, but you'll have more fun. And you'll be the benefactor of a large inheritance.

Who knew project planning could be so much fun?
So get writing, get brain dumping and get EXECUTING!
I'll see you at your country pile.

GETTING STUFF DONE LESSON 2:
BEAT ANALYSIS PARALYSIS

YOU'VE GOT YOUR to-do list in place now. Hell, you've got your whole LIFE planned out and you're determined that NOTHING, not even the beak-nosed interfering of your sister-in-law, is going to get between you and your dreams.

But you've fallen back into the trap of making simple really difficult.

You're thinking too much. You are PARALYSED by your insistence on OVER-ANALYSING every path of action you consider.

You're suffering from Analysis Paralysis.

Analysis Paralysis is the debilitating state you get yourself into when you insist on looking at every possible outcome of any variant course of action. You end up looking at so many fluctuations and permutations and potentialities that you lose the ability to get started on anything.

Analysis Paralysis is an illness that commonly affects corporate institutions, where decisions are made by committees who insist on feasibility studies, cost/benefit models and 18 signatures before the toilets can be cleaned.

Analysis Paralysis also afflicts folk who are looking for good excuses not to do the thing that they say they're going to do.

- 'Yep, I'll look into it.'
- 'What would the consequences be?'
- 'I've got to speak to my husband.'
- 'Let's do the numbers.'

These are all examples of the debilitating symptoms of an acute attack of Analysis Paralysis. Being able to make a decision will help you massively in this, and you can do that already, can't you?

Here are some tips on beating Analysis Paralysis and being just about the most awesome individual to ever walk God's earth.

1. EAT AN ELEPHANT.

Even if you're a militant vegetarian, you started your elephant eating[12] during the last chapter when you put your life plan on paper.

---

[12] For those of you who haven't wasted your youth learning elephant-related metaphors, this has nothing to do with 'the elephant in the room', which deals with glaring issues that aren't being addressed and everything to do with the solution to the problem that is eating an elephant, which is to consume it one bite at a time. This means you need to break a big issue down into manageable chunks.

By breaking an issue down into its component parts, it looks less scary and more achievable.

2. FUCK PERFECT.

Perfection Infection is the older brother of Analysis Paralysis. You might be able to convincingly conquer the latter, only to be royally buggered by the former.

This happens because you start stuff, but you're AFRAID of finishing stuff – or calling it finished – unless it's *just right*.

Have you ever locked yourself in your bedroom and refused to come out to greet your dinner-party guests because your fennel and camembert souffles refused to rise?

Probably not, but you see where I'm going. If you're afraid that *delivery* can only happen when you've got a world-beating product, plan or souffle, then you'll be waiting a long time.

Forget perfect and learn to make do.

By settling for 'good enough', you'll free yourself up for a little more fun, a little more spontaneity and fewer malicious whisperings behind your back.

3. DO LESS.

Don't do stuff for the sake of it. Trim, prune, cut back, decimate, CHOP.

Fifty per cent of the stuff you do doesn't need to be done. Do you NEED to go shopping for NEW STUFF when you should really be GETTING RID OF STUFF? You already own too many shoes. Half the shit in your kitchen cupboards is perfectly edible but hasn't been touched in weeks, so you can skip your trip to the supermarket. You never even got round to opening the last 18 books you bought, so don't go on a book-buying trip.

What about that to-do list you're going to write? It's the eighth one this week. Do you need to write it? Or will you just ignore it like the last one? Either do what you're going to do, or don't do it. Don't plan and plan and plan. Just do it.

You don't need to take on whatever you're taking on. You only THINK you need to do what you're about to do.

BANG! Fifty per cent of your day reclaimed.

4. TAKE LONGER OVER STUFF.

Yes! OK, revelation coming:

MOST DEADLINES DON'T MATTER.

See that thing you need to do? Put it off until tomorrow. What's the worst that can happen?

You: *'Oh golly, I really need to bake those pumpkin and goats-cheese tartlets or the world will fall apart.'*

Me: *'No it won't.'*

Now, it's not OK to let people down, so don't promise what you can't deliver, even pumpkin and goats-cheese tartlets. But the less you promise, the more time you win, the more you deliver.

51

BANG number two. You now have more time for personal hygiene, going to the gym and French-kissing.

You rock.

GETTING STUFF DONE LESSON 3:
THROW OUT THE TV

SO, YOU WANT to GET MORE DONE in LESS TIME? That's good. That's the kind of incentive that will get you on the right path to your perfect life, the one that involves long Mediterranean lunches, a fatter bank account and holidays in unpronounceable places.

The good news is, there's a single, simple and EASY step to getting more shit done in less time. It's not difficult. There isn't a single one of you out there that can't manage it.

In addition, the knock-on effects go beyond getting stuff done and ticking boxes. The associated benefits of implementing this ONE little step are manifold and include a better love life, more quality time with your kids, getting into better shape and improving the acid reflux that has dogged you for the last six years.

If you're the kind of person that reads self-help books (hello!), then you'll have a million plans for the kind of stuff you want to do with your life. They include, but aren't limited to:

- Homeschooling your kids
- 60 minutes pre-dawn inverted yoga on weekdays. Muffins on weekends.
- Rearing your own organic piglets for company and lunch
- Penning a fictional biography of Egon Schiele
- Delivering a series of lectures on sustainable corporate social responsibility
- Knitting your own carbon-neutral mode of transport
- Setting up Cornwall's first holistic spa for retired race-horses
- Writing your soon-to-be bestseller: *Tug of War – a history of military masturbation*
- But something keeps getting in the way.

Your plans remain just plans, scribbled down on various bits of paper that end up in various lint-lined pockets, on bedside tables and underneath those books on better parenting, better dietary habits and more effective non-verbal communication that you read but never implement.

'*The problem is,*' you say, '*the problem is that there aren't enough hours in the day. What with taking the kids to their golf lessons and the dog to the dry-cleaners I don't get a minute to myself. By nine o'clock when the kids are in bed, and I'm exhausted, it's all I can manage to not fall asleep in front of the TV.*'

Yeah, yeah, yeah. WHATEVER.

So here's the solution to not falling asleep in front of the TV and freeing up three hours of time in your day that you didn't have before. Here is the single and only thing you have to do in order to create more hours in the day than you currently spend on your commute:

THROW OUT THE TV.

That's it. And it's easy as taking a dump. So do it.

Get rid of the biggest lump of techno-distraction that ever darkened your otherwise quite light and airy doors.

THROW OUT YOUR TV.

Seriously, do it NOW. Unplug the TV, put it in a fucking hole in the back garden and never look at it again.

'*But but but but but...*' you say. '*But but but but...*' you say before I interrupt you with an enormous TRUTH:

If you do what you've always done, you'll be the same fat, underachieving whiner you've always been.

So throw out your TV.

Have you done it yet?

No?

OK, I can wait.

Done it now?

Yes?

Good.

(Liar)

So here's the concrete result:

Your free time to work on patenting your veterinary-goose-inflater, forming your Hungarian chopstick orchestra or reverse-engineering the CT scanner has just increased MASSIVELY.

Where you once only had 30 minutes snatched between Wilhelmina's Peruvian pottery lessons and Rupert's opera surgery, you now have AT LEAST THREE CONTINUOUS HOURS every day to Get Stuff Done.

Not convinced? Are you happy with the way you spend your downtime?[13]

If you are, and defend to the death your right to rot your brain, think now of your epitaph[14].

Would you rather:

'*Inventor, writer, industrialist, innovator, polyglot and lover*'

Or:

'*Knew the names of the girls on* UK's Next Top Model'

Yep. Thought so.

[13] Because it's OK to chillax and do nothing. It's OK – I mean that. But YOU have to be convinced it's OK as well. It's no use saying to yourself that it's OK, but secretly loathing yourself with each extra minute you spend in front of *I Used To Be A Celebrity On Love Island*.

[14] Your epitaph is the stuff they write on your gravestone: devoted father, lover of animals, largely present husband etc.

GETTING STUFF DONE LESSON 4:
SEVER YOUR COMPUTER CABLE

WELL DONE. You've salvaged three hours a day and are getting six times more done because the idiot box that took up half your living room is now being eaten by worms and pissed on by badgers in a hole in your back garden, under six feet of soil.

Best place for it.

But there's other technological nonsense that gets in the way of your getting stuff done and enjoying life to its full, creamy, orgasmic potential[15].

Your computer.

That's the little plastic box of bytes that sits malevolently in

---

[15] Because you *do* deserve to enjoy life. If you've been brought up to believe that life is about work and sacrifice and that the rewards come later in some distant utopia about which there exists no empirical evidence, then you need something I can't offer you here. Get to a deprogramming centre sharpish.

your living room and possibly your bedroom and maybe even your kitchen if you're in really deep.

In fact, you could be from one of those families that have one computer per person, plus at least one more for the household. That's pretty normal now and pretty modern. But remember to talk to each other using your mouths at least once a day.

It's no surprise that aimless surfing of the internet[16] sucks more hours from your day than taking tea with Great-aunt Jemima and her collection of doilies.

It's true that as a productivity tool the internet is pretty hot. It can save you hours if you use it properly. You can order your groceries online, which saves you a sweaty trip to an out-of-town supermarket populated by extras from *Star Wars*.

If you're banking online, you don't have to queue at the neglected, piss-stinking High Street branch behind 18 octogenarians counting out their coppers and cashing in their pensions.

And of course the internet has liberalised the market for pornography. Some quality girl-on-girl-on-dwarf action can now

---

[16] Incidentally, dude, you are not SURFING the internet. There is nothing LESS like surfing than clicking away masturbatorially on your mouse for hours on end. Surfing is an energetic outdoor activity performed by flaxen-haired and brown-skinned dudes with enviable physiques. Excessive internet use is the primary domain of lank-haired, bottom-heavy teenagers who are unlikely to recognise the outdoors unless it's displayed in pixels.

be purchased for no more than a couple of clicks, saving you both money and the embarrassment of the wagging tongues at the corner shop.

Yes, the internet has its benefits.

But it's also the biggest time-suck you ever let into your house since you agreed to a demonstration of the PowerSuckCleanRight Modular Vacuum Cleaner. It's a vortex, a black hole that swallows minutes and hours and trades them for Repetitive Strain Injury and a slight, persistent headache.

You know how it works. You sit down to send a quick email and get momentarily distracted by a HILARIOUS video of a kitten climbing a ladder to the Benny Hill theme tune that was sent to you by some kid you went to school with but didn't ever talk to except to steal their lunch money. Then, when you next check, it's four hours later and all you have to show for it is a memory of a baby biting his brother's finger, a subscription to a raw-foods newsletter and a credit card charge for eight pairs of anti-slip tights and a colon-cleansing kit.

And you haven't had any dinner.

WHAT A PHENOMENAL WASTE OF LIFE.

So curb your internet use and gain more hours per day.

Here's how you do it.

1. WHEN YOU'RE PLUGGED INTO THE INFORMATION SUPERHIGHWAY, APPLY THE SAME (ADMITTEDLY LAX) STANDARDS OF BEHAVIOUR YOU'D APPLY TO YOURSELF IN THE REAL WORLD.

This will work if a typical day for you doesn't entail standing in front of the window of an electronics shop and watching repeat episodes of *You've Been Framed*, announcing to hundreds of people simultaneously that you've just had a 'yummy avocado and brie ciabatta' for dinner, then conducting a survey of total strangers about the best way to get back with your boyfriend.

That's what the internet is for.

2. USE YOUR OWN NAME.

This prevents you from logging into forums and embarking on misguided arguments with people you've never met about the merits of Justin Bieber over the Spice Girls. You're not going to have that conversation in real life, so don't have it in the ether of the internet.

3. SET YOURSELF A TIME LIMIT.

It's a rare luxury that we get to walk into a friend's house when they're not home and get to rifle at leisure through their bedside cabinets, underwear drawer and the little room under the stairs where they keep the Hoover and the shoe polish. It will only be a matter of time before they come home and we have to act like we're not remotely interested in that kind of stuff. Our natural curiosity will be curbed by the real-life application of the ticking clock.

Similarly, when you're stuck at the office, time-wasting opportunity is normally limited (unless you're a civil servant). You've got to clock in and clock out and arsing about can only be done on your 20-minute tea-break.

Unfortunately, the same rules don't apply to the online world. It's a great big timeless playground where, if you're not military in your planning, you will lose the day.

Do those three things. Give yourself a half-hour limit or 45 minutes or whatever. But if you find you're spending less time interacting with your family than you are playing online poker, something's got to give, and fast.

GETTING STUFF DONE LESSON 5:

GET YOUR SORRY ARSE OUT OF BED

YOUR SOCIAL LIFE is no longer unsocial. You don't watch TV, ever. Your click, click, click time is limited to half an hour a day. You've got your life back!

Now GET OUT OF BED AND MAKE THE MOST OF IT.

The third SECRET to prolonging your day and making light of the limited time you've got left is to GET OUT OF BED.

You have to sleep. You should sleep whenever you can. But when you're done sleeping, GET UP!

The benefits of getting up early include:

- Hitting the street before the neighbourhood dogs have crapped all over it.
- Getting in to work earlier to rifle through the HR woman's staff files to find out why Dolores has taken so much time off work recently.

- Having the time available to ignore all of the stuff you feel that you're meant to be doing and indulge yourself stupid with the extra two hours you've created for yourself. Read the newspaper on the toilet, write a love letter to your next-door neighbour's wife, build a scale model of the Eiffel tower out of breakfast cereal and toilet paper. The possibilities are endless.

But waking up early can be a bitch. And even worse, if you've managed to actually *wake up*, is getting your sorry arse out of bed in order to do something with the day.

The single best remedy to oversleeping and wasting hours fiddling with yourself under the duvet is to have kids. For the first 12 years of their lives, they'll *guarantee* that you can't sleep in even if you want to.

In the beginning, there'll be crying to soothe and nappies to change, then there'll be breakfast to supervise, fights to break up and injuries to tend to with sticking plasters and kisses.

But kids aren't an easy solution to implement, unless you're a 15-year-old girl with an older boyfriend and a White Lightning habit, and then they're easier to end up with than herpes (although you'll get that as well).

Kids also represent unique time-management issues and you'll find that getting up early *because* of kids means that your day is spent tending to them. You've never been more productive, but your productivity is centred on bottle-warming, sick-cleaning and bum-wiping activities.

You claim it's tough to get up in the morning, but you never have difficulties if you *need* to get up. How many times have you missed an early-morning flight? Not many, I'll wager.

So that's the key to getting up. Spend money on an appointment that you can't afford to miss, and schedule it as early as you can. Or tell your boss that you'll be in his office at seven o'clock. You're not likely to phone in because you 'overslept', are you?

It's the simple and easy conundrum again. Make the simple intention of getting out of bed and eating breakfast and leaving the house easy to implement.

Litter your house with alarm clocks, get your mum to call you on the phone. Do whatever it takes, but get out of bed.

Nothing beats the feeling of ticking off the last item on your previously created to-do list and realising it's only half past nine in the morning.

Just imagine: you can have your first martini at 11 o'clock.

GETTING STUFF DONE
LESSON 6:
GET HELP

WHO DO YOU think you are? Superman?

GET SOME HELP!

You don't really believe that the best way of doing whatever it is you've got to do is alone, but you like to think of yourself as an 'independent woman' or 'a man who can'.

Your distorted sense of pride is stopping you doing one of two things:

- Asking for help; and/or
- Accepting help when it's offered.

Take the following situation, one we can all relate to:

Your prize-winning collection of koi carp need to be vaccinated against seasonal flu. You've got two hundred of the buggers and they're slippery customers. Getting hold of them is one thing, let alone keeping them still long enough to vaccinate them.

You devise a method of doing it and estimate that it will take you five minutes to net, jab, tag and release each fish.

(5 Minutes) x (200 fish) = Fucking Ages

And, as the icing on the cherry bakewell, you have a dinner planned with your sexy estate-agent in five hours' time.

Here's how you do it:

Get five people to help you.

BANG! Seventeen hours of work distilled into four. Your sanity saved and the prospect of shacking up with aforementioned sexy estate-agent tripled, thus guaranteeing a lifetime of spiritual harmony and breakfast in bed.

Simple, huh?

And the *real* beauty of this trick is that it doesn't apply only to inoculating expensive fish.

Shopping, housework, envelope-licking, data-entry, house-building, holiday-planning and all manner of getting things done can be made shorter and more enjoyable by accepting help.

If you don't have any friends to help you, move directly to Part Four of this book that addresses just that.

Do not be proud. Take a moment and realise, amigo:

You Can't Always Do It On Your Own.

If you haven't got any friends or if your friends are as useless as you, it's time to get the professionals in. Move swiftly to the next chapter. Do not stop for a cup of tea.

GETTING STUFF DONE
LESSON 7:
OUTSOURCE

YOU HAVE A responsibility to yourself to concentrate on the cool shit. Admittedly, you probably still have to go to work, unless you're a trust-fund baby or benefit cheat. Work sucks, but it's what we have to put up with to finance the cool shit.

And what is this cool shit?

It might be easier to say what it *isn't*. Cool shit isn't ironing, laundry, upholstery, washing dishes, mowing the lawn, shining your shoes or doing your accounts.

Not unless that's exactly how *you* define cool shit. In which case, that's cool. It's great that de-creasing and blanching and starching and steaming and sweeping turns you on. I can even understand it a little. There is something therapeutic, after all, about polishing the family jewels.

But for most folk that's not cool shit. Cool shit is sitting around a country pub with eight of your closest friends as a bearded barman pours you flagons of mead. Cool shit is kicking back with the girls over a bowl of noodles after an outing to *Sex And The City 6: Carrie Gets Her Varicose Veins Done*. Cool shit is building dens out of discarded pieces of corrugated plastic; playing football with dog-turds for goalposts; reading naughty books about the travails of Szechuan sex-workers; taking a bath with your husband's brother and shocking the local chapter of the Women's Institute with sordid tales about you and Petru the Corsican barkeeper.

You're already doing more of the cool shit because you've freed up hours in your day by getting rid of your TV, cutting the digital umbilical cord that ties you to the internet, hauling your arse out of bed two hours earlier and roping your friends in to help you with the carp immunisation.

Now you're going to take it to the last level of splendid. Applying this last technique is like hitting the Big Red Button. This is not for beginners. This is the nuclear option, the one that will leave you feeling like you're having your back rubbed by Ying the masseuse while all the shit that isn't cool gets done around you.

That's because you WILL be getting a back rub while all the shit that isn't cool gets done around you, because you're not going to be doing any of it.

The secret to effective implementation of the stuff that you don't want to do – whether it's tax returns, ironing, defrosting the freezer or worming the dog – is to get somebody else to do it.

DELEGATE and watch your workload drop.

And you don't delegate to begrudging neighbours and reluctant family members. If you do that, they'll think they're doing you a favour – or worse, they'll feel coerced – and you'll end up owing six hours of reciprocal tedium and backache the next time one of them moves house, or baking an apple and apology pie to make up for a deficit of goodwill.

No, forget your friends and family. If you're going to delegate properly, you need to delegate to complete strangers. And you need to PAY people to do the stuff that isn't compatible with your rock-star life.

After all, that's why you work, isn't it? You work so that you can look after your family. That means, after covering their unreasonable demands for food, shelter and clothing, you need to spend time with them.

To spend time with them, you've got to spend less time scrubbing the bathroom.

Nobody looks back on the innocent, endless days of their youth and says, 'Our house was spotless!' They say, 'Remember the time we were going to set fire to the cat out of sheer boredom, but then Mum and Dad took us to watch *Jurassic Park* instead? That was awesome!'

And if you haven't got kids, the same applies. You have to spend most of your day in the office. So why work when you get home? Wouldn't you rather be drinking gin and creating salacious gossip or eating cakes or learning how to fly horses?

For a few quid, you can pay somebody to come and hoover your dog, shine your carpets and clear away the collection of funky tissues that are stuffed down the back of your teenage son's bed. It will take them about three hours. And for that, you get to avoid clearing up after yourself for at least four days of the week.

I'm not talking about tasking EVERYTHING out to somebody else. Your finances won't let you, most probably. But at least start with the bits that you really hate.

Perhaps the weekly trip to the supermarket zaps you of the will to live, and you'd rather pull your toenails out than have to stand in line next to women with tattoos and men with earrings?

In that case, draw up your shopping list and send somebody else. You can use the extra hour and a half you've just won to have a yoghurt and mint facial.

Or perhaps it's the thought of mowing the lawn that makes you throw up a little bit in your mouth?

Great, there's an easy solution. Pay some young dude to do it while you finish your compendium of space-travel-themed poetry.

'*Oh,*' you squawk, '*but I couldn't possibly. The whole concept of domestic help is so repellent to me. It harks back to darker, colonial times when house-boys were kept on as punkah-wallahs for their bewhiskered masters and kept on standby for emergency gin and tonic administration. I couldn't possibly put another human being into domestic bondage!*'

Get over yourself[17].

There are thousands and thousands of eager, hard-working individuals out there who would love for you to spend some of your hard-earned money on paying them a salary.

Whatever it is, whether it's buying your husband's birthday present, or coming up with the idea for your husband's birthday present or even jumping out of a cake and BEING your husband's birthday present, there are people and organisations out there that can help you.

'*But I can't possibly afford to have staff,*' you say. '*I don't earn nearly enough money.*'

Perhaps you're right. But if it was a job that you couldn't do yourself, even if you wanted to, like retiling the roof or rewiring the boudoir or fumigating the attic, I bet you'd find the finances somewhere.

The resources are in you, you've just got to allocate them properly. Your two main resources are time and money. Both are valuable. Spend them wisely.

---

[17] If you do manage to change your views by listening to the compelling and persuasive arguments that follow, then be sure to embrace your new stance wholeheartedly. If you do not, you risk becoming one of those people who cleans up before the cleaner arrives and says, 'I'm not cleaning, just tidying.'

GETTING STUFF DONE LESSON 8:
APPLY THE EIGHT MINUTE RULE

WELL DONE. You're outsourcing the really soul-destroying tasks and you're roping in friends for the time-consuming ones. That leaves the rest.

These are the little things that you leave to accumulate. You don't do them when you have the opportunity and you end up having to schedule big productivity surges. These tasks and jobs and errands build up like little balls of energetic stress in the kitchen sink or under the stairs or in the bedroom.

You let this collection of little stuff grow until you flip. Then you embark on a frenzy of activity, getting things done, cleaning cars, getting to the dry-cleaners, writing your thank-you notes, disinfecting underwear, before repeating the cycle over again the following week.

Boom and bust.

These bipolar bursts of activity rock the steady foundations of

73

your coasting along as the suave man-for-all-seasons you aspire to be.

You want to be the kind of host that can offer a gin and tonic to a friend that drops by at no notice, in an apartment free from piles of laundry and cat hair, and from a kitchen that isn't doubling up as a petri dish.

But you can't find the time to do the laundry and clean up the cat hair and you always forget to buy tonic.

But here's how you can get all that shit done in *only a fraction* of the time you've freed up by chucking out your TV[18].

Pick your tasks one at a time and apply:

The Eight Minute Rule

Most of the things that need doing around the house can be done in under 10 minutes. That's a really short period of time. If you have your snooze button set to 10-minute intervals, you'll appreciate just how little time that is.

BUT. It's enough time to do LOADS of stuff:

- Taking out the rubbish – 2 minutes
- Loading the dishwasher – 4 minutes
- Vacuuming one room – 7 minutes
- Ordering your week's supply of gin and tonic – 4 minutes
- Ironing two shirts – 8 minutes
- Going around your bedroom, picking up every stray sock

[18] You have chucked out your TV, haven't you?

and T-shirt and chucking them all in the laundry bin –
3 minutes
• Paying the electricity bill – 6 minutes

If you've got young kids, eight minutes is about the maximum time you get to yourself anyway. Load the washing machine in your first eight minutes, and drink that gin and tonic in the second.

When you get home tonight, after boiling the kettle and in the eight minutes that you would have had before *EastEnders* started, DO SOMETHING. It won't take long (under eight minutes, in fact), you'll experience the warm glow of achievement and you'll be one step closer to being the domestic goddess you aspire you to be.

GETTING STUFF DONE LESSON 9:

THE BOTTOM LINE:
DO SOMETHING NOW!

STOP PUTTING SHIT off. Do something now.

Shoes need shining? Do it.

Rubbish needs taking out? Do it.

Washing up? Do it.

Don't even read to the end of this chapter. Stop reading now and do whatever it is that you need to do.

NO EXCUSES.

Don't stop to think about what it is that you need to do, just pick something and do it. Don't spend hours sorting and organising and shit, just get on with one single thing. Now.

Things you CAN do now include:

- Pay some bills
- Phone a client ⸺⸺⸺ ✕
- Clean your desk

PHONE A CLIENT

- Get some laundry done
- Go for a run

Things you CAN'T do now include:

- Coffee break
- Cigarette break
- Phone a friend
- Suck your teeth and look into the middle distance.

If you get TWO things done today, that is TWO more than yesterday.

MAN! You're on the way to achievement!

Get stuff done. Stop reading this. Do something.

See you tomorrow.

GETTING STUFF DONE
LESSON 10:
OR DO NOTHING

THIS IS THE alternative to Doing Something.

You may well have got this far and thought, '*What the hell? I thought this whole book was about taking life less seriously. I thought that, if I didn't want to do something, then that's OK. What's this whole chapter been on doing stuff? There's a ton of stuff I DON'T want to do. Is that OK?*'

Of course it's OK. You have to decide what's got to be done and what doesn't have to be done. You're only responsible to yourself, unless you're married or living with somebody, in which case you're responsible to other people as well.

In many cases, you might find that you are actually responsible *for* a lot of stuff that happens to the other person in your marriage. Should your wife, for example, get her heel stuck in a drainage hole, do not be surprised if you find that you need to shoulder a little responsibility. If she loses her house keys, don't pretend you had nothing to do with it, even if you didn't. And if she spends more money than she could possibly earn in three months on a particularly shiny pair of shoes with a killer heel and a little ribbon which was an absolute MUST HAVE because the blonde woman in that American show about girls and sex was wearing a pair? It's your fault for not giving her enough attention.

Also, if you have kids or family or friends you actually care about, then your responsibilities are a little broader than if you're just living alone with a collection of Japanese pornography and a pinball machine.

So, if you have read the previous chapters and said, '*What the fuck – I need validation for all the shit I'm NOT doing,*' then I'll give it to you. There. You've got it.

You don't NEED to make sure that the light-bulbs in your home are functioning. It's entirely up to you if you want to live in a house with overflowing rubbish bins and a colony of ants vying for space with rats and urban foxes.

But be honest with yourself. Is that what you want? Probably not.

Of course, I might be wrong. You may be a true nihilist. You may see your wallowing in insect shit and mouse droppings as your God-given right. Perhaps you're making an environmental statement. Perhaps you want to sleep with the pest-control woman who's called to your slum once a week when the neighbours complain that the rats have grown to the size of rabbits. In which case, OK.

But that's not the case, is it? In fact, you sense a little frisson of self-loathing each time you catch sight of your toothbrush which hasn't been changed in four months, or the soap-dish that houses pubic hair and spittle.

Get a grip, man, for God's sake.

You need to redefine what's important and act on it, and doing the little things that aren't immediately enjoyable are a little important, because they allow you to do more of the big things that really rock.

But if you want to take this one step further and you really want to do NOTHING that doesn't involve basic survival, then perhaps this is you:

You get up each day, eat your breakfast and head off to work. You want no stress. You'll do what your boss tells you to do because that keeps life easy. On Fridays you go out with the guys from work and shoot pool and drink a few beers.

The weekends are for leisure and recreation. Leisure and recreation are the most important things a man can do with his life[19]. You go fishing, you drink a few more beers, you play a bit more pool.

You hang out on the beach.

I think, my friend, that you may just have it sussed.

Because – and I'm being DEADLY serious here – because that's

---

[19] Especially when he's young. Just be sure to wear protection. Nothing can trample on your plans quicker than an unexpected pregnancy.

what most of us are striving for, isn't it? The kind of stress-free life where we don't have too many concerns, where the boss doesn't shout at us and we enjoy time with our buddies, shooting deer or playing rugby or hanging out in saunas or whatever it is that rocks our boat.

There's a story that you may have already heard about an American businessman and an Antiguan fisherman. It's a long story and I'm not inclined to repeat it here[20].

The summary version is as follows: there's a young fisherman dude. His life revolves around catching fish for a few hours in the morning, then kicking back with his family, listening to some reggae, smoking some dope, sinking some ice-cold beers, kicking a football around barefoot on the sand and whatever other stereotypes of young Caribbean males you can conjure up.

An American fisherman sees him hauling his catch in one morning and asks a few questions about the commercial viability of an industrial fishing fleet and then maps out the next 20 years of this young fisherman dude's life.

It's an attractive proposal at first glance. In return for equity in the company and his fishing expertise, the businessman will invest

---

[20] Actually, I'm not repeating it here because I can't track down who wrote the thing in the first place and I want to avoid any thorny copyright issues. I'll be worth millions one day. Don't want them all stolen from me by some cash-hungry charlatan on the basis of having used one of their lame stories in my book. In fact, that's going in my next book *How To Get A Grip On Copyright And Intellectual Property Issues* and its sequel *How To Get A Grip On Frivolous Lawsuits*.

in him to muster a small army of fishing vessels. They'll grow to become a publicly listed company and the little dude will be able to retire, after 20 years' hard toil, at the age of 40.

'And what will I do then?' asks the little Caribbean dude.

'Then, little Caribbean dude,' replies the American businessman, 'then you can retire to Antigua, catch some fish and hang out with your family.'

In short – it's OK to do what you're doing now, if you're happy with what you're doing now and you're not pissing on anyone's parade.

It's OK, even if you're doing nothing.

PART THREE

DEALING WITH OTHER PEOPLE

LATER ON IN the book, you're going to learn about relationships; real relationships with important other people. You're going to learn about the kind of relationships that involve emotions and bodily fluids and arguments about whose turn it is to take the bins out.

But first you need a crash course in communication.

Communication is the science of talking to other people or writing to them or sending text messages and smoke signals. In order to live with other people (which you do, unless you've eschewed the vagaries of society and chosen to suck moss in a cave while ranting about government thought-control experiments and chemical Armageddon), you need to talk to them.

It's not always easy, but there are ways of coping.

These are just some of them.

DEALING WITH OTHER PEOPLE LESSON 1:

DON'T BE SO SENSITIVE

DO YOU FIND yourself getting easily offended by the words and actions of others?

Are you quickly irked, miffed or put out?

Do you tut-tut and write angry letters of complaint to newspapers and television stations?

Do the following situations make you go a little bit mental inside:

- Blasphemy?
- Kids with hooded tops smoking in designated non-smoking areas?
- Bad language on the television?
- People who should really know better turning up to the golf club in tie-dyed jeans and lurid pink Hawaiian shirts?
- Your mother-in-law faintly damning your choice of curtains?

Yes?

Get a grip.

Stop your sensitivity habit now. What are you, addicted to drama? You need to blow up at the smallest provocation to keep life interesting? You're an attention whore? What is it? What's your motivation?

Just stop it DEAD. Over-sensitivity will kill you. It will cause you stress and stress is the single largest cause of death among otherwise healthy men and women the world over[21]. You worry, you die.

Seriously, when did you last enjoy any concrete, tangible benefits from getting put out?

What about that time the waiter spilled duck consomme on your slacks? You got angry. It wasn't a big deal, but your reaction to an entirely UNIMPORTANT event beyond your control got you irked and turned what should have been a decent lunchtime catch-up with an old buddy into a slightly awkward backwards and forwards with the catering staff about a dry-cleaning bill.

Here's what happens if you find other folk's behaviour distasteful or if some random occurrence which really isn't significant rocks your world in a bad way:

- You get upset, your blood pressure gets raised, you lose a

---

[21] This may not be true.

lot of time worrying and you shave seven minutes off your own life.

- Nobody else gives a shit.

Now, IT DOESN'T MATTER what others think, granted, and crucially, you're not qualified to determine the thoughts of others, but, when you get upset by what other people do, that's what happens:

YOU get upset. And that's it.

There are a lot of things in life worth fighting for and getting pissed off about. You can legitimately be offended in the following instances:

- Bob looks you square in the eye and says, 'You're a useless waste of space.'
- Gerald tells you he thinks your kids look like they've been dragged through the ugly bush, backwards.
- Ernie borrows £100 and tells you he has no intention of returning it.
- You see your name in a newspaper under the headline 'This person is a nonce.'[22]

People generally aren't out to offend you. If something somebody says makes you twitchy, ask yourself if you can put

---

[22] You may only be upset in this instance if you are not, in fact, a nonce.

it down to ignorance, stupidity or that form of Tourette's syndrome that courses sporadic profanity. The answer is usually yes.

Ask yourself this:

'*Was the intention of that person's actions to cause me offence or is he just somebody who doesn't do things the way I do things?*'

The answer is normally: '*No, that person's intention wasn't to cause me offence, therefore I won't get upset.*' Other people are stupid. Put it down to stupidity. You can forgive that, can't you?

On the few occasions that the answer is '*Actually, yes, I think he did want me to take offence*', then don't take the bait. Smile and nod and say something mildly patronising but largely innocuous.

Don't give any of those bastards the satisfaction of seeing you upset.

If you're still inclined to take issue with something, because your life is incomplete without drama, then so be it. I'm not here to tell you what to do, dickhead.

And while your decision to not get miffed over something somebody else says or does is all very brave and good and estimable, it ignores the underlying key to the whole point about dealing with other people:

WHAT OTHER PEOPLE THINK ISN'T IMPORTANT[23].

---

[23] This comes off as a little selfish. But it is true, most of the time. If you're a half-decent human being, there will be situations where pleasing people is your top priority. And, unless you're a callous misogynist, the reasonable demands your wife makes on your time should be catered to.

If Bob thinks you're a useless waste of space, so be it. See ya, Bob. Have fun hanging out with other people.

But unless Bob actually *tells* you that's what he thinks, how do you know that's what he's thinking?

Your summary assessments of what's going on the minds of other people are WRONG more than they're right.

Take these examples:

SITUATION #1

You're walking down a BUSY street, full of cool kids hanging out and listening to their ghettoblasters and sipping frappuccinos. You're carrying your groceries, nonchalantly whistling and then BANG! You slip on an artfully placed dog turd. You fall flat on your derriere, shopping goes everywhere and you split your lip.

You think:

'Ohmygodohmygodohmygod I look like such a DICK. Ohmygod I'm COVERED IN DOG SHIT and everyone can see that I buy cheap groceries. Ohmygod ohmygod I will NEVER survive the embarrassment and humiliation and will forever be associated with the shitty slip in the middle of the street. OHMYGOD MY LIFE IS OVER.'

Everybody else thinks:

'Poor thing. I hope she's OK.'

SITUATION #2

You've finally plucked up the courage to invite the sexy librarian out to dinner. After months of flirting over Keats, Byron and Bryson, you swallowed your male pride, taken action and invited her out and OHMYGOD she said YES! You've spent two hours in the bathroom, scrubbing your crotch with disinfectant and reapplying your HoldItFast Hair Wax three times. You've ironed your best shirt – the one without yellow stains in the armpits – and you're looking pretty darn HOT when you catch a final glimpse of yourself in the mirror. OHMYGOD! You've got a HUGE ZIT just below your nose. But it's too late to do anything about it. The taxis waiting downstairs. Bugger. You jump in the cab, sit down to dinner and watch the evening spiral into disaster.

You're thinking:

'*Shit! My chances are totally blown here. She's thinking I'm a total LOSER, bringing a frickin' SPOT to dinner. But it won't be here blotting my visage forever, so I'm not going to mention it. I'll studiously ignore its existence and will casually cover it with my hand while making scintillating conversation to salvage the situation.*'

She's thinking:

'*He seems like a really hot, intelligent guy. The kind of guy who I'd like to take home and suffocate with my thighs, but I wish he'd stop rubbing that tiny little spot below his nose. It's getting redder and redder.*'

SITUATION #3

You're at the coolest bar in town. You've drunk half a bottle of champagne and have spent the last two hours snorting coke off a toilet seat with an advertising executive you've just met.

You think:

'OHMYGOD I am on BRILLIANT FORM. I'm looking good, feeling good and my conversation is just SCINTILLATING. I'm a confident and forthright young person in the prime of my life and the best raconteur you ever met. I'm going to do a tour of the room to introduce myself to everybody.'

Everybody else thinks:

'What a dick.'

* * *

In each situation, you've been wrong and hopelessly so. In fact, you're wrong more often than you're right.

When it comes to other people's thoughts, you have NO IDEA what you're talking about. You are uniquely UNQUALIFIED to offer advice to yourself pertaining to the whirrings and clickings between the ears of people that aren't you.

So don't.

Focus on YOU. Focus on the bits you can control. You've got your list of what's important and what isn't. Focus on the important stuff.

Don't be so sensitive, it will kill you. And when dealing with other people, find out exactly what they're thinking by asking them. They should tell you straight.

DEALING WITH OTHER PEOPLE LESSON 2:

NOBODY TELLS ALL THE TRUTH, ALL THE TIME

SO.

'… *find out exactly what they're thinking by asking them. They should tell you straight.*'

But that's the problem with 'should', isn't it? It doesn't mean what it says.

You ask folk to tell you straight and they won't. They'll avoid and evade and wriggle.

SHOCKER: People don't tell the truth all the time. *(Nor do you.)*

They fib and they lie and they disappoint. *(So do you.)*

But you're not bothered! No! You've already lowered your expectations and avoid disappointment by having this situation well and truly licked.

The truth is, we're all driven by an intrinsic awareness of the need for self-preservation. That means we will adapt what we say to suit the situation.

You lie to yourself all the time. You say, '*I'll go to the gym tomorrow*' or '*I'll stop smoking*' or '*I'm not going to check my emails over the weekend*' or '*I'm really interested in postmodernist architecture and will read more about Frank Gehry*' or '*She won't mind if I have another pint.*'

You will agree, therefore, that, because you lie to yourself so readily and brazenly, you can't expect others to be truthful with you.

Even the people who love you the most will lie to you. Remember when you were a kid, and your mum would come and watch your end-of-term ballet performance, then tell you how wonderful you were? Well, sweetheart, she didn't think you were wonderful. She didn't enjoy herself one bit. Of course, she was *pleased* to be making you happy, but the actual *performance*?

Rubbish!

And, although her eyes didn't leave the stage once and they were glued to you the entire time you were dancing, the overriding thought running through her mind was: '*Perhaps we should try horse-riding next time. She really sucks at this ballet shit.*'

We lie to be kind. And we lie to protect ourselves.

- '*No officer, I thought I was well within the speed limit.*'
- '*I didn't buy this mobile phone off a kid on the Tube.*'
- '*I graduated from my degree in Water Treatment Plant Operations with honours.*'
- '*I am the best man for the job.*'

We men lie about our alcohol consumption all the time.

When we were young, we would boast about our liquor-holding skills and tell you we'd sunk eight beers in one sitting, when really we'd only had three. We needed to keep up with the boys. Now we're older and married with kids. Consequently, when we've been in the bar all afternoon, we'll always say we only had two pints.

It doesn't mean we don't love you.

But the people you don't know so well? Don't believe them. Make your own decisions about people and what you think of them and don't base them on what they want you to believe.

Anybody who tells you how awesome they are before you've had a chance to figure it out yourself may not be all they're cracked up to be.

Trust your judgement and don't always expect the truth or you'll be disappointed.

DEALING WITH OTHER PEOPLE LESSON 3:
SAY WHAT YOU MEAN

DEALING WITH THIS deluge of dishonesty is difficult. You can't control what others say or how they think or act, but you *can* control what YOU say and how you act.

Learn to talk straight and say what you mean. It might start a new craze.

At the moment you're a wet lettuce. You're afraid to be direct. You have a tendency to constantly flit around important issues or sidestep difficult questions.

You find yourself saying, '*No, that sounds great*', when you really mean, '*Urgh… I'd rather rearrange my facial features with a spanner.*'

The consequence of not standing up for yourself like the biped with a backbone that you are is that you spend your days pleasing others and neglecting yourself.

This advice is for you:

SAY WHAT YOU MEAN!

The number of hours in the day is finite. There are nominally 24, but, once you've arsed around washing dishes, anaesthetising wasp stings, changing nappies and hiding from Big Dave the Debt Collector, the useful hours in the day are considerably fewer.

In addition to all the time-creating devices you took on board previously in this book, you can make your time count for more by starting out on any course of action with brutal and unremitting honesty.

If the question is:

'Would you like to take a ride in my SUV and spend the afternoon picking wild mushrooms for an organic supper?'

Then the answer is:

'Yes' or *'no'*, depending strictly upon what your decision actually is. That's the only criterion[24].

'Would you like?' means nothing more than *'Would you like?'* You either would like or you wouldn't like. If you can think of nothing greater, then say, *'Yes.'* If you really don't want to go fungus-foraging, then say, *'NO.'*

You can qualify your answer[25]. If you're going to do that, be direct as well.

'The thought of spending the afternoon with you is an attractive

---

[24] There's also a third option, which involves your not being able to make a decision, but we covered that in the first section and you're now decisive and firm and committed. Well done you!

[25] Whenever you read the words *'You can'*, be sure to respond with a *'Too bloody right I can. I can do just about anything I feel like, thanks very much.'*

one. However, I can think of a dozen things more interesting and exciting than mulching around in the damp for toadstools. Let's go ice-skating instead, then I'll buy us pizza and we can throw stones at empty beer bottles.'

BRILLIANT! You've not only carved out an infinitely more interesting Saturday afternoon for yourself, but you've also stamped some of your own character on to the proceedings.

And similarly, if you don't really fancy going on a mushroom hunt, but you know that doing just that would make your counter-party immeasurably happy, and that is more important to you than ice-skating or pizza or avoiding an afternoon foraging, then, on balance, your answer is: 'YES, I would like to do that', albeit for reasons that weren't immediately obvious to you.

DEALING WITH OTHER PEOPLE LESSON 4:

THE GRASS IS ALWAYS GREENER, INNIT?

IF YOU FIND that the grass is often greener, it's time to buy some fertiliser.

Let's be literal about this for a moment. You live at number 62. Your front garden looks like it may have been transported from Calcutta. There are three bin bags, one shopping trolley, three-quarters of a car, and much of last night's dinner obscuring the ground. If there is any grass on your side of the fence, the police are interested.

But just next door, at number 64, the garden looks like gardens are supposed to look. There is a lawn, the lawn is green and made of grass; there is even a gnome. The gnome looks contented. You have never seen a happier gnome. The gnome is doing fucking cartwheels and singing little songs about what a happy gnome he is.

You decide, with your tautological wisdom, and through a

particularly laborious decision-making process, that in order to get your garden to look like next door's garden you need to move next door.

So you move next door. Within six months, your garden looks like shit.

Do you see what I'm getting at?

So let's be less literal. Forget about the actual herbaceous border, and let's have a look at the other tangibles.

Your neighbours at number 64 are Reg and Anne-Marie. Reg runs a bovine castration company. Anne-Marie is a lady who lunches. In addition to her lunches, she is an author who has churned out a semi-successful series of trashy airport romance fiction. In addition to this, she is the chief organiser of the monthly Neighbourhood Watch meetings, president of the recycling association and the governor of the local primary school. She bakes a mean apple pie and practises mixed martial arts.

Despite being so busy, Anne-Marie always looks good. When you bump into her in the street, your bedraggled hair clinging greasily to your nylon top and your camel toe starting to itch, she'll be perfectly perfumed and coiffed.

You say, '*Gosh, Anne-Marie at number 64 is always looking so good. Her hair is always perfectly permed, her shoulder pads exactly the right height and her skin is a truly enviable shade of nutmeg. She clearly spends time choosing her clothes, her makeup and her selection of handbags. I so wish I had Anne-Marie's life.*'

But you know the reason, the real reason, why Anne-Marie at

number 64 is always looking so good with her perfect home and perfect shoulders and her perfect tan.

You don't?

Let me help you. You think it's something to do with genes? You think she was born with shoulder pads and a bronze face? Of course she wasn't. The reason Anne-Marie's metaphorical grass is so much greener than yours is because she waters it.

So here's the secret to the greener grass, a more efficient company, a better relationship with your husband, a higher daily rate, more beautiful fingernails and the ability to afford expensive vacations.

You have to work at it.

Stop making comparisons, because comparisons make you miserable. Focus on your own garden and buy some fucking fertiliser.

DEALING WITH OTHER PEOPLE LESSON 5:

HOW TO COMMUNICATE

'OK, OF ALL *the chapters in this book, this is the one I need the least. How to communicate indeed! What's this guy doing? Trying to insult my intelligence? I've got half a mind to climb inside the pages of this bloody book and punch him on the nose.*

'*How to communicate?! I know how to bloody communicate! Open my mouth; let people know what I want, and BOSH! I'm in with the win. And not just basic communications, either. I'm Chief Negotiator of Negotiators R Us. There's nothing you can teach me.*'

Yes – it's true. You're an awesome speaker, aren't you? I remember when you were just a nipper, talking in complete sentences by nine months and using polysyllabic sentence constructs by 12 months. You wrote a dissertation on the inadequacy of formula milk before you stopped drinking it.

And when you joined little school you were always given the role of narrator in the nativity play, because that was the one that had the most lines. And you memorised them. And you memorised every other part, so that when Joseph peed his pants on stage and had to be replaced you jumped in and did his part for him, better than him. That was your first standing ovation.

At secondary school you joined the debating society. Who can forget your award-winning defence of the motion that 'This house believes that the Commonwealth is an antiquated and defunct institution'? I remember it well, particularly as the opposing team had fallen ill with food poisoning after a dodgy serving of semolina and you had to step in for them at the last minute as well. Really! Arguing both sides of the debate with little preparation! A real tour de force.

You were made head girl and when speech day came around your oration was delivered with poise, grace and humour. You had the Lord Mayor rolling in the aisles and five minutes later the Lady Mayoress was wiping tears from her eyes as you told of the orphanages you had visited in Eastern Europe as part of your Brilliant Young People of Britain training.

You're so smooth and so convincing and so bloody *persuasive* that you've won regional salesperson of the year six years in a row. You use your 'Wonderful way with words' to get your point across and you're a fantastic conversationalist, aren't you?

You're always invited to dinner parties because you're a scintillating conversationalist; the 'life and the soul', they say (although you cringe at the cliche), with an opinion on everything. You read voraciously and make sure your day always begins with the *Today* programme. God forbid you should be short of an opinion when called upon.

And yes, you talk a lot, but that's what you're known for. You're loquacious, garrulous and verbose and you make no apologies. What is life for if not for communicating?

And so what if the less strong talkers get edged out? So what if the weaker members of the tribe can't get a word in despite their best efforts? Social intercourse is a test of strength and you're fucking Hercules!

But you forget to listen and your monologue is tiring your friends.

Shut up for a minute and listen.

LISTEN!!! LISTEN!!! LISTEN!!!

And shut up.

DEALING WITH OTHER PEOPLE LESSON 6:

HOW NOT TO BE A DOORMAT

UNSPOKEN CONTRACTS AREN'T worth the paper they're not printed on.

'*If I rub her back for 16 minutes with lavender oil, then I'll get a blowjob*' is only a sure thing if it's been agreed upon previously and there's no allergic reaction to the lavender oil.

Here's the thing: people won't always do what you expect them to do.

You have this idea that, if you do X, Y and Z, then the rest of the world will automatically owe you something and you'll have this fantastic life of people giving you shit because you've done good stuff.

Yes, it's true that, if you tend to be a giver, you'll also get given cool shit in return. It's the law of reciprocity. And it exists.

But there's a difference between giving a lot and being a total fucking doormat. How many women make dinner for ungrateful husbands who do nothing more than moan that their fish fingers aren't crispy, or there's too much ketchup in their crisp sandwich?

If you don't set up clear 'give and take' rules, you'll find that you do a lot more giving than taking.

Yes, good people tend to attract good people, but some good people end up being weirdo magnets, hassled on the Tube and robbed blind by slick-scalped smooth-talking con-men.

If you hold the door open for somebody you don't know, you don't have the right to be pissed off if they don't smile and say thanks.

Why should they smile and say thanks? Did you agree it with them beforehand? Or did you just expect it of them because that's what you understand the immutable laws of etiquette to dictate?

Get a life. We've all got our own moral codes and scruples. And, if you're me or you, and if the correct response *is* to smile and say thanks when somebody holds the door open for you, because that's what our moral code dictates, then hooray. But if you're not me or you and you're one of life's ignorant pricks, then you might not say thanks. And you might not smile. And you might even resent this random act of goodness.

You don't know what other people are thinking, remember. Christ, half the time you don't have a clue what YOU are thinking. How can you expect anybody else to know what perfect combination of successive events you've got planned out in your meticulous brain?

For example, if you've decided that the best way to leave work early on Friday night for your parents' 70th wedding anniversary is to pull an all-nighter on Thursday, but you haven't already cleared this with your boss, then don't be surprised if he doesn't agree. In fact, if you then insist on leaving early *because* you worked late, that's nothing short of being a manipulative arse.

Imagine, just for a second, that you need a new car. You go to the dealership and you tell the dealer that you're in the market for a Satsuma coupé. He shows you the latest model, boasts about its walnut and cream interiors, lets you take it for a test drive and then gives you coffee as he discusses payment plans.

At the end of his energetic and inspired presentation, however, you're still not convinced. You tell the salesman you're going to think it over. Then you get a bill for the coffee, petrol and half an hour of the salesman's time.

Do you pay it?

Of course you don't; it wasn't part of the deal.

He may *expect* you to pay it, but, because he hadn't told you that the price of the coffee, petrol and patter wasn't included in the presentation, you don't think it's fair.

Forget thinking that the world is made up of Jedi mind-ninjas. It's not. People need to be told what to do.

If you want a seat on the bus but some dude is taking up two seats, the way to get the seat is to say, 'Excuse me, I'd like to sit there.' You don't get the seat by tutting and moaning and sighing and casting filthy glances at the person in the way of your ultimate goal.

That's called passive aggression, and it's the insidious enemy of straight talk.

DEALING WITH OTHER PEOPLE LESSON 7:
HOW TO TALK TO STRANGERS

STRANGERS: YUCK, EH?

Avoid them! Kill your intellectual curiosity and shut yourself off from interesting opportunities by not talking to strangers!

After all, what did strangers ever do for you? From youth it's been drummed into us that talking to strangers is a recipe for abduction, anxiety and tooth decay. (Although on the plus side there were plenty of opportunities for seeing puppies.)

Talking to strangers, or hell, even making EYE CONTACT with strangers, can cause you all sorts of damnation. You'll be invited to obscure events, you'll be trapped between people you have no interest in talking to at dinners you don't want to be at, you'll be pestered for opinions and asked for favours. Can you spare £500 for corrective surgery? Will you watch my Doberman while I go for a pint? Can you launder this dirty money for me? Christ! Is there anything worse?

I think not. Talking to strangers is BEST AVOIDED.

After all, you're happy with who you know, aren't you? Your circle of friends is sufficient. The last thing you need in your life is MORE BLOODY PEOPLE. You've enough of the pesky blighters knocking you up for sponsorship money, dinner invitations and babysitting duties as it is. You don't want to get any more of those, thanks very much.

You're sending a clear message to the world, and that message is LEAVE ME ALONE.

But what if that wasn't the case? What if engaging in polite chat with people you don't yet know led to general life-enhancing goodness. What if, by speaking to somebody you've never met before, you enlarge your horizons and open doors? Doors that were previously closed to you. Doors that lead to the discovery of new joys and undiscovered experiences? Joys like spelunking, archery, cartography and late-night roadside copulation?

So this is this chapter's little suggestion: spark up a conversation with somebody you don't know.

It doesn't need to be terrifying. If you're the type who would sooner rearrange your facial features with a blunt instrument than chat to someone you don't know, don't worry. You're not alone.

In fact, there are only a *very* few of us who find it comes naturally to talk to somebody in the queue for the salad bar at a wedding. It doesn't feel right, does it? God, the shame of somebody muttering, '*I'm sorry, have we met before?*' The mortifying blank stare, silence and an awkward shuffle away from you.

So what's the worst that can happen? You might be making a friend of an escaped psychiatric patient, but apply a little common sense and be prepared to back-track – and run – and that won't be an issue. You might be mistaken for a mugger, which means your victim will be doing the running. If you're really lucky, they might chuck their wallet at you as they're hot-footing it away. *'Take whatever you like,'* they'll say, *'just don't hurt me.'*

Result.

No, the worst that can happen to you is summary rejection. You can deal with that, though, because you're getting a grip.

Here's how you talk to strangers:

1. IDENTIFY STRANGER

Good strangers to identify are generally fully clothed, not engaged in conversation with themselves or an imaginary friend. Their limbs are largely non-flailing and you can't smell their hair from 10 paces. Ladies in high heels with peroxide extensions who hang around unlit corners after dark will be happy to talk to you, but it will come at a price.

Good places to talk to strangers include aeroplanes, post-office queues, coffee shops and parties. Less ideal environments are cinemas and the front-row seats at funerals.

2. ONCE YOU'VE IDENTIFIED THE STRANGER, SMILE.

Do this briefly. Make eye contact, briefly. Do not grin and nod your head enthusiastically.

3. IF YOU ARE NOT MET WITH AN ICY STARE, OR SCREAMS, SAY SOMETHING.

Good things to say include:

- 'Hello.'
- 'How do you know Bob?'
- 'Is anybody sitting here?'
- 'Boy. I've had a long day. It's good to rest my weary toes. What about you? Have you come far?'
- 'Can you help me? I'm wondering if I should buy the blue or the green dressing gown. My normally excellent dressing-gown taste-radar has gone into melt-down and I'm having trouble choosing.'
- 'Excuse me, what exactly is the difference between tofu and Quorn?'

Slightly riskier things to say include:

- 'Have you ever seen a dead body?'
- 'Can you smell shit?'
- 'What's the square root of 957?'
- 'Can you hold this cheese for me? I'm late for the bookmakers

> *and the bastard still owes me forty quid. If he doesn't pay up,*
> *the court is going to revoke access to my kids again.'*

- *'You look just like my stepmother. She used to beat me. I've*
  forgiven her, but it took eight years of therapy and electric
  shocks. Don't worry, though. I'm much better now. And you
  don't look that much like her.'

If you get a positive response, carry on.

A decent response is an answer. An excellent response is an answer that includes a question. That's what salesmen call a buying signal. You have the green light to carry on.

So carry on. Ask open-ended questions, or tell a story.

If you find it's not really going anywhere, it's OK. You can say, *'Thanks, enjoy your flight'* or *'I'm going to get another whisky'* or *'Oh, look, somebody who wants to talk to me'*, then make your excuses and leave.

However, if you find that you've had an absolute blinder of a chat and reckon you've made a new friend, find a way to follow up.

A great, non-freaky way of following up is to connect people.

'Wow, you're a fashion historian? That's fantastic and guess what? My friend Augustus is really into pre-Byzantine fashion and is looking for a historical dressmaker for a project he's working on. I think the two of you would get on and he's really cute. Let me put you in touch? Do you have a card?'

'If you're serious about getting your teeth fixed, let me send

you the name of my teenage daughter's orthodontist. What's your email address?'

'I think you're really cute, but I'm married. I have a single friend, though. Let me put you in touch.'

BANG! You've just communicated with another human being and there's one less stranger in the world.

Say goodbye to an old age filled with cats and ready-meals. Say hello to a lifetime of PARTY.

IMPORTANT INTERLUDE:
HOW TO TAKE YOURSELF LESS SERIOUSLY

THIS IS AN INTERLUDE, an intermission, a little *pause*.

Intermissions, whether at the theatre, cinema or dancing macaque cabaret, give you the opportunity to take a leak, smoke a cigarette, eat an ice-cream and stretch your legs. You can compare notes with friends on Gustave's interpretation of Beethoven's ninth and make a quick phone call to the babysitter to check that Hortensia hasn't swallowed the cat. In short, intermissions are designed for relief.

This brief intermission in *How To Get A Grip* is designed to provide you with the ultimate relief: relief from yourself.

Boy, do you need it. You follow yourself around everywhere.

So relax, put some reggae on the ghettoblaster and roll yourself a big fat spliff.

Thanks to a scientifically designed[26] programme that follows,

---

[26] I got a B in GCSE physics.

over the next five days the single biggest problem you have is going to be addressed and resolved. It's more important than learning to communicate, clean your house more quickly or getting more hours in the day. It's more important than all the other stuff we've dealt with so far.

This issue addresses YOU. Solving the problem of YOU will eliminate STRESS from your life, which is necessary because stress kills.

Dealing with this problem is your key to wealth, health and happiness.

The issue I'm talking about? It's the problem of taking yourself too seriously.

Taking yourself too seriously is the quickest route to boredom.

The quickest route to taking yourself too seriously is to worry about shit that doesn't matter.

Therefore, a guaranteed way of being bored with yourself and everything you do is to worry about all the stuff that you don't have to worry about. With me?

So if we agree that anxiety = boredom = self-loathing and ennui, then we agree that it's of the UTMOST importance that we deal with it immediately.

STOP EVERYTHING AND DO THIS! THIS WILL SAVE YOUR LIFE!

DAY ONE:
DANCE NAKED

I'M ENTIRELY INDIFFERENT about public nudity. That said, I'm inclined to verge towards discretion. If you're already a nude rambler or naked sunbather, then that's great. If you have a penchant for whipping your kit off and wiggling your bits at people *who haven't asked to see them*, then you're likely suffering from a personality disorder or a distinct and serious lack of empathy.

Shared nudity needs to be consensual. So, on this first day of your interlude, you need to consent to seeing yourself naked. I'm not asking you to share your pale, pasty flesh with anybody else (although if your wife or husband wants to join in, then it's a bonus for everybody).

Once you've got your clothes off, you're going to dance in front of a mirror. And you're going to do it with joyful enthusiasm.

This is about being comfortable with your body, one element of your life that you're guilty of taking too seriously.

Nobody likes *everything* about their body. Perhaps your ears stick out or you've got a paunch. Perhaps you've got an unsightly third nipple or a little dent where your left kidney used to be. For some of you it will be cellulite, or a caesarean scar. For some of you it will be man boobs and a chunky double chin.

Well, guess what? You're not alone. EVERYBODY has an issue. Anybody who says, 'I'm entirely happy with my body' is either lying or a Premiership footballer.

So GET OVER IT.

I'll wager that the last time you took your clothes off and had a really good boogie was a long, long, long time ago?

You might find dancing totally naked a liberating experience or you might find it mortifying, but, once you catch a glimpse of yourself with a shit-eating grin and your bits bouncing bountifully, you'll find it tough to suppress a smile.

So here's what you need to do:

Make sure the doors are locked and the blinds are down. Find a big mirror. The one in your bedroom on the wardrobe door is a good choice. The one in the shopping mall is a bad choice.

Turn up the heating.

Put something funky on the stereo. Something that you'd dance to if you had your clothes on, had sunk four shooters and were out with the girls on a hen night in a nightclub on the end of Eastbourne pier.

Now, take your clothes off. All of them. Don't leave the G-string or the boxers on. This is no time for modesty.

And now the fun bit. Dance as if nobody's watching. (Hint: nobody is watching, unless you're have seriously determined neighbours or a landlord with illicit camera installations.)

Dance like it's going out of fashion. Dance like you've got to dance just to survive.

Do the hand jive, do the funky chicken, do a one-man conga. Just dance. Let yourself go.

When you're ready to stop or when the song finishes, start all over again.

Why this works:

NOBODY has ever been able to take themselves seriously with their dangly bits dangling and bouncing about to the sound of Gloria Estefan and her Sound Machine.

And what a sense of liberation! Nothing else matters. It's impossible to think about other stuff when you're playing the pink air guitar and head-banging. I challenge you to worry about your bills when your boobs are knocking you in the face and you're performing the splits.

Don't worry about your stubbly legs. Don't even think about your love-handles. Celebrate your imperfections and remember what it was like to be a teenager.

Dance naked and be free.

DAY TWO:
GET MESSY

YOU'RE A CLEAN freak. So we're going to deal with this today.

On the list of things that are important, temporary levels of personal cleanliness are way down at the bottom. Longer-term considerations of hygiene and personal representation come into play if you sustain dirtiness for any period of time, but a brief detour to the land of grub is going to break down your fear of not being altogether presentable.

If you're terrified of having a rollicking time rolling around in the park because the prospect of grass stains terrifies you, then you need to do this. If you carry an alcohol-based hand sanitizer around with you in case of dirty door handles, you need this even more.

Your body is resilient. Your body can cope with a bit of grime and a handful of germs. Your immune system is geared towards self-preservation and unless you're into German love-games then you're not putting yourself in any grave danger by getting a bit mucky.

Kids love getting messy. You stopped enjoying it when you started spending money on your own clothes. Your attachment to your Gucci loafers has taken precedence over your ability to really *let yourself go*. So let's remedy that right now.

If you live in the country, find a puddle and jump in it like a six-year-old. Find some dirt and smear away. Put on some shoes that don't cost three hundred quid and go and destroy them. Roll around. It won't kill you.

If you can't get messy outside, perhaps you live in the city or perhaps you're afraid of toxoplasmosis[27], then get messy at home. The kitchen is the best place for this. Or the garage. Smear yourself in oil. Smear yourself in flour and water. Get some of that posh chocolate body paint and cover yourself in the stuff.

And then head back to the mirror. Look at yourself. You're grubby. The facade of your Rimmel foundation and Toni and Guy hairdo has been slightly chipped away at. You're human. You're messy.

---

[27] The nasty little parasite in dog-shit that makes you sick.

DAY THREE:
SING LOUDLY IN PUBLIC

AAAAH, THE SWEET beauty of self-expression! Opening your mouth and singing out loud feels SO GOOD, doesn't it?

You KNOW you love to sing, even if you're shit at it. When nobody's around, in the privacy of your own home, you love to have a little warble. Perhaps you even sang a little bit on Day One while you were prancing around your apartment in the nude?

You sing in your head ALL the time. You hear a song you know, either a catchy one or a less catchy one that's become ingrained in your subconscious through repeat exposure (Bryan Adams' 'Summer of '69', for example), and you sing along with it, whether you mean to or not.

Or you leave the house in the morning and the last song you heard on the radio stays lodged in your memory and stuck on repeat until the joker from the helpdesk swans into the office humming the theme tune from *The A-Team*, which takes its space.

But you never sing in public. Perhaps after six vodkas and lime you might be tempted, but you rarely succumb.

So start to be honest with yourself. You love to sing and you can't stay locked up at home all the time. So take yourself out of the house, quit suppressing the inner chorister, and sing your little heart out.

Walk down the street – resist the temptation to wear headphones – and sing. Do it loud and do it wholeheartedly. Don't stare people out, but don't avoid eye-contact either. Sing like you're happy and smile with it. It's easier when you're walking, but, if you feel like doing it in the middle of the mall, that's OK as well. It's only one step up from whistling to yourself, and nobody blinks when you whistle.

This bit's important: DO IT ON YOUR OWN. Don't stroll out with your girlfriends, linked at the arms and crooning along. That's chicken. The power of this exercise is to do it without the support network.

And this bit's important as well: don't do it drunk. Do it stone cold sober, first thing in the morning. Sure, it will help if the sun is shining, but, if it isn't, sing 'Singing in the Rain' or 'Raindrops Keep Falling On My Head', or that depressing tune by Travis.

You can dance as well if you like. It's optional. It's a lot of fun. I recommend keeping your clothes on while you're dancing in public though. There's a difference between putting yourself outside of your comfort zone and getting arrested for offending public morals.

Sing loud and sing proud. You'll find it addictive.

DAY FOUR:
SEND SOME FAN MAIL

YOU'VE GOT OVER your phobia of dirt, you've sung in public and you've danced naked. Now write to a stranger.

Write a letter to somebody who doesn't know you and tell them something nice.

Choose somebody in the public eye. They're used to receiving letters from folk less reticent than you and will be less inclined to think they might have a stalker.

Tell them how much you admire their shoes or their teeth or the way they dealt with the rumours about their love-life and the gerbil.

And then go one step further and tell them a secret. It's good to share and easier to share private stuff with people you don't know very well.

If you're unsure what to write, try this:

Dear Famous Person off the TV,

I wanted to drop you a quick note to let you know that I had my verrucas frozen off last week.

You might not see that this is relevant to you, but it is. While I was waiting in the doctor's surgery (a little bit scared, to be honest), I read an interview with you in one of those slightly outdated glossy magazines that you often find in waiting rooms.

There were pictures of you and your wife, both dressed in flowing white linen and lounging around your stately home, stroking shaggy-haired children and throwing balls for pristine Labradors.

I'm not ashamed to say that I lost myself in your wonderful world for a few moments, and I'm quite sure that the resulting positive rush of endorphins went some way towards alleviating the pain of the liquid nitrogen being applied to the soles of my feet.

So, Famous Person, I want to say a big THANK YOU for having a positive impact on my day.

Kind regards,

Etc, etc

The reason this works as a tool for taking yourself less seriously is because your carefully constructed facade of cool won't allow you to play fanboy or fangirl to folk you admire from afar.

But try it. You might even get a reply.

Then you'll be *really* excited.

DAY FIVE:
WEAR FANCY DRESS

DAY FIVE AND you're so nearly there! You've got rid of your body issues and had a good boogie, you've got over your dirt phobia, tackled your fear of sounding like a prat and learned that you don't always have to play it cool.

Now we're going to deal with not caring that we LOOK like a fool.

You put far too much stock in your appearance. Remember how you don't know what other people are thinking? And remember that what other people are thinking doesn't matter? Well, it applies to what you look like more than ever.

You remember when your heel broke and you were MORTIFIED? There was no way of getting it fixed quickly and you had to wear your tennis shoes. Remember how bad it felt?

(But remember how comfortable you were for the rest of the day?)

Or the time at your cousin's wedding when you spilled ketchup all down your chocolate-brown Hermes tie? And you had to borrow a tie with cartoon characters on from your dad? Do you remember how MORTIFIED you were then?

(But also remember how you still got to know the bridesmaid pretty well?)

You attach far too much importance to playing it cool.

Hopefully, by now, you'll have been playing it so un-cool for the last few days that you'll be looking forward to this last step.

Today you need to source some dressing-up clothes and go somewhere public and busy. You could dress up as a ballerina or a clown or a large teddy bear. Avoid the man-kini and keep your boobs covered: you're not aiming for arrest on charges of indecency.

Then, once in your cowboy outfit, or your Ewok mask, head to the post office. Join the queue and buy some stamps. Go to the supermarket and stock up on the week's supplies of tangerines and cod liver oil. Have a coffee.

You may be challenged by Very Important People who demand to know what's going on. A security guard may collar you and sneer with undisguised contempt at your outfit and outlook.

If asked, '*What's all this about?*', you reply, '*What's all what about?*' If asked, '*Why are you wearing that costume?*', you reply, '*What costume?*', and, if approached by a gang of young rat-faced men with a can of lighter fuel and a box of matches, run like it's going out of fashion.

And then get home, run yourself a bath and get out of your hippo outfit. Stop a little while and have a naked jiggle in front of the mirror. Remember how good it felt? Lie back, hum yourself a tune and write yourself a letter in your head about how much fun you are to be with.

And to think you'd almost forgotten how to enjoy yourself.

PART FOUR

RELATIONSHIPS

NOW THAT YOU can deal with other people, you've got to accelerate those skills.

Statistically, you're likely to derive some satisfaction from meaningful relationships with significant other people. There are the people we choose: our friends and lovers; and there are the people that we're stuck with whether we like it or not: our family.

At some stage in your life, you're likely to want to graduate from heavy petting and move into a relationship based on trust and shared responsibilities and a commitment to having it off even if you don't really feel like it.

You may find you want to have children. You may not be able to have children. You may get stressed about the prospect of moving in with each other or getting your foot on the property ladder. You might have to deal with the shit-fight that is disapproving siblings or argumentative parents-in-law.

In short, relationships can fast derail anybody who has previously held a very firm grip on the stuff of life.

This part of the book will help.

RELATIONSHIPS LESSON 1:

IT'S NOT WHO YOU KNOW, IT'S HOW YOU TREAT THEM

FEELING A BIT down? A bit isolated? A bit lonely?

And you've no idea why? It really shouldn't be the case. You're investing in relationships like it's going out of fashion:

- You've got 4995 folk connected to you on Facebook.
- Your Twitter follow count is in the low thousands.
- You have a little black book that's FULL to bursting with digits and names and contacts.
- You have a shoebox full of business cards.

Congratulations.

You give all these folk the time they need – a smiley here, a retweet there. 'You Like This.' You send a bit of fan mail and you get all giddy when Ashton Kutcher @replies you.

But who are your friends?

(Not the kind of friends who say 'ZOMG ROFL LOL'. Not the kind of friends who say '*You rock!*' The kind of friends who say '*Tell me more, I care*' or '*That was a stupid thing to do, but I still love you.*')

If you're hanging out with the cool kids online or giving each person a blink of an eye's worth of attention or climbing the greasy soiled rungs of the ladder of *arrivisme*, then do something different this weekend.

Un-neglect your friends. You need friends. You will never be homeless if you have a true friend and you'll never have a true friend if you neglect them.

It doesn't take much, it really doesn't. A phone call on their birthday is sufficient, a postcard from your holidays[28], an email that says, 'I was just thinking about you.'

Don't let this happen:

'*I've been meaning to get in touch with her, but it's been such a long time that I feel guilty about facing up to the fact that I haven't called. She'll think I don't care. It's best to stick my head in the sand and forget about it.*'

Sound familiar? This is how relationships fizzle away into nothing.

So follow these steps. RIGHT NOW.

---

[28] I know these are going rapidly out of fashion, but for my money anybody who takes 15 minutes out of their snogging and sangria holiday roster to write me a postcard is a fucking legend.

1. Think of a friend you haven't spoken to in a few months.

2. Pick up the phone and call him.

3. Start the conversation like this: '*Hi! How are you? It's been ages? What's going on?*'

4. Set a date for a follow-up – a coffee, a meal, another phone call.

5. FOLLOW UP!

There, you've just salvaged a sinking relationship. That is seriously cool.

Treat your friends well and they will treat you well.

Treat your friends like they're dying.

RELATIONSHIPS LESSON 2:
HOW TO TREAT PEOPLE

'TREAT YOUR FRIENDS like they're dying.'

WTF?

Yes, really. Imagine that the next time you see them will be at their funeral. Imagine that you'll NEVER see them alive again. Imagine that NOW is the only chance you get to leave your definitive mark on their lives.

You'll treat everybody better.

'Live every day as if it were your last' is typical advice for making the most of the days you have. That makes sense. An attitude like that encourages you to do the fun stuff, not to worry too much about the less fun stuff and focus on having a good time. If you're not going to be here tomorrow, you're going to speak fondly with the people you love and make peace with people you don't talk to any more.

But if you live EACH day like it's your last, then it soon

becomes unsustainable. It becomes unsustainable because, once you've only got 24 hours left on the clock, the threat of consequence diminishes into nothing. You can do *anything* and there'll be no fall-out.

This would be great if it really *was* your last day, but it isn't[29].

You'd tell your boss to lose his stapler up his oversized backside. You'd drink whisky for breakfast and have unprotected sex with your neighbour's 22-year-old daughter. Without the fear or threat of the law, you'd rob banks and parade naked in public, reveal all your best-kept secrets to the Sunday newspapers and behave as disgracefully as you wanted to, without the prospect of hangover or imprisonment. Hell, you could get arrested just for the fun of it.

So, if you did that each day, you'd burn out pretty quickly. If you live each day like it's *your* last, the emphasis is on YOU. You'll act selfishly because the consequences have disappeared.

But, if you live each day like it's EVERYBODY ELSE'S last day, then you're on to a winner.

If life is about having fun and connecting with good people, then how better to give your full focus to the cool kids around you than to imagine them in your life for only a fleeting moment?

Treat them like they're dying.

Don't be morbid. Don't cry and sniffle. You don't have to handle everybody you meet with kid gloves or prop their heads

---

[29] It may be. I really don't know.

up on their pillows and sob audibly when you leave the room. But imagine that the folk you meet today – the folk you love and care about – won't be here tomorrow. You'll change the way you treat people for ever.

If today is the last opportunity you'll have to see everybody you know and love, how will you treat them?

When people die, you think about your last interaction with them, your last meeting or phone call. And then you kick yourself silly for months and years if you didn't say all the stuff you wanted to say – all the true stuff, all the soppy stuff – before they snuffed it.

You had a fight with your best friend and two weeks later she was hit by a bus.

You fell out with your mum a year ago because she called your wife a stuck-up whore. Sure, she was out of line, but you kind of hoped you'd make up one day. Now she's dead and you didn't even say goodbye.

That shop assistant who short-changed you absent-mindedly three months ago lost her job when you complained to her boss. She couldn't pay her rent and ended up homeless, succumbing to starvation and hypothermia three months later.

Take a moment to think about all the folk you love: your wife, your mother, your husband, your father and your kids.

Now imagine that they won't be here tomorrow.

Tell your wife you love her. Play with your kids. Call your parents.

Treat them like they won't be here tomorrow. One day, they won't[30].

---

[30] That said, it's perfectly legitimate to piss people off from time to time. Remember, people are sensitive (especially the ones that haven't yet read this book). But a caveat: should you find that you're pissing everybody off all the time, you need to stop being a dick.

RELATIONSHIPS LESSON 3:
WHEN TO COUPLE UP

YOU'RE NOT UNHAPPY, are you?

Your life's pretty FUCKING good, actually.

You wake up with the sun, your head is clear and your focus is sharp. After 90 minutes of Bikram yoga, a cold shower and an alfalfa body scrub, you grab a quinoa and spinach smoothie at the Tibetan café on the corner of your gated street and stroll into work.

You catch a glimpse of yourself in the window of the vintage second-hand shop where you occasionally go to pick up squirrel-fur moccasins. HOT DAMN you're looking GOOD! YOU ARE FINE! The pricey bridgework on your molars was worth the eight grand you dropped on it to have a Hollywood grimace. Your abs are sculpted yet discreet and your clothes whisper, 'I've got money AND sophistication.' Your skin glows without shining and your hair, a careful blend of salt, pepper and cumin, shines without dripping.

You get to work and, BOY, your job ROCKS. You're on the creative team at Goldmeister, Platinum, Dope and Awesome, London's freshest advertising agency. You can't call it work, not really. It's more like a day playing truant from the asylum. You breeze in soon after 10 o'clock, kick back, drink an organic soy latte with Hermione the funky receptionist who hides her classical good looks behind oversized spectacles, then spend 15 minutes shooting the shit with a crowd of SERIOUSLY COOL late-twenty-somethings who wear drainpipe jeans, trainers from two decades ago and improbable hairstyles.

Lunch is a pretty chillaxed affair, normally hemp bagels with wheatgrass and bulgur extract, some sustainable salmon and Nepalese yak's cheese. You eat it perched on a translucent bar-stool on the agency's roof-terrace, watching the vapour trails tickle the capital's skyline and feeling pretty damn smug.

Dinner comes early. You make small talk with clients at a private members' club in the West End. These guys are your friends, you'd hang out with them even if you didn't get paid. Two caipirinhas, a game of pool, some sushi that's been flown in this morning from Osaka, and an early taxi home. ALL ON EXPENSES. You're not sure life gets better. In fact, you've got a boner at the prospect of tomorrow.

Home is EXACTLY what you intended it to be. It's a temple to everything you represent. There's an enormous yet almost invisible plasma screen in the corner, framed with limited-edition pop-art prints by your favourite Lebanese artist. Your games room is air-conditioned and filled with American pinball machines from the 1980s. There's a space-hopper in the corner. Your bathroom is finished with bamboo, slate and little limestone Buddhas, all pointing towards the bedroom (excellent feng shui). Your towels are by Hugo Boss.

The fridge is stocked with bubbly and Eastern European beer, and there's six bottles of Grey Goose in the freezer for the odd occasion that your friends drop round for PlayStation and blinis.

You jump into bed (Egyptian cotton sheets, natch) and take a deep, meditative breath.

Yes, you lucky bastard, life doesn't get better than this.

So why are you so fucking lonely?

You've got everything. But you haven't got company. You haven't got that one person that is the difference between *having it all* and *having enough*.

It's time to fall in love.

RELATIONSHIPS LESSON 4:
WHY YOU NEED A PARTNER

THE LITTLE NAGGING voice has convinced you that need a partner. This is good.

LIFE IS BETTER WHEN YOU SHARE IT.

You might resist this. *'No, I resist this,'* you might say. *'I like my own space and my own life. Some of us are meant to be alone. I am one of those people.'*

Bollocks. You are only a few years away from a house filled with cats. A nurse will wipe your incontinent arse in old-age because you have no family to look after you.

You NEED a partner. Don't fight it, hombre. I'm right on this one.

The benefits of being in a relationship:

- When you notice a cat narrowly avoid death at the beak of a particularly vociferous oversized seagull (an infrequent occurrence and one that needs remarking upon), you have somebody you can turn to and say, '*Did you see that?*'

- After having accepted a generous offer from Stacey to attend her hen night at the tequila factory, you inconveniently find yourself in need of somebody to help you keep your hair out of your face as you reacquaint yourself with projectile vomiting. You are grateful that your boyfriend is on hand to perform such an unpleasant task uncomplainingly[31].

- When you've fallen out with your best mate Ken over something stupid, and possibly related to computer games, and you've missed your sales targets at work which means you'll be passed over for promotion, and you stub your big toe on the way from the bathroom, you spontaneously burst into tears. You haven't cried in years and you surprise yourself and it makes you cry more. When this happens, you'll be grateful to have your lady on hand to wipe your eyes, make you a cup of tea, make you feel better and NEVER TELL A SOUL.

There are even tax advantages.

By now you're convinced, yes?

Good. You've made a great decision. You want to fall in love. Now, in an ideal world, cobber, you'll fall in love with somebody who loves you back, or at least quite likes you.

Let's start looking.

---

[31] By the time your boyfriend becomes your husband, this task will no longer be performed uncomplainingly or without considerable recompense.

RELATIONSHIPS LESSON 5:
HOW TO FIND A PARTNER

REMEMBER THIS:

You can't choose who you fall in love with, but you can choose where you look.

The last three guys you've been with haven't been ideal.

1. Lenny 'Hard' McHard: muscled, macho and protective. He let you know how much he valued you by dishing out physical 'justice' to anybody else who looked at you, or thought about you or he thought might have been thinking about you. You decided to end things with him when he suggested a tracking device. He still sends his boys round 'to make sure you're OK'.

2. Johnny Nonchalant: laidback to the point of falling over, which he often did. You loved his *joie de vivre*, his focus (or lack of focus) on concentrating solely on the real fun shit.

Washing up, ironing, working for a living, taking showers and paying taxes were all 'Just a bit too much hassle, man.' Boy, he was refreshing and frequently stoned. You left him after you lost the best part of three weeks that you'll never get back. He didn't even notice.

3. Steve the Fence: a real charmer. He said all the right things and devoted hours and hours to you. There were expensive meals in restaurants with knives and forks, there were trips abroad to visit his family in Marseilles and Sicily and who could forget the impromptu speed-boat trip down the Thames? It was like something off a film. But Steve's best quality was his ability to get you the perfect gift. So lavish! So generous! So thoughtful. You only had to mention the latest Ernesto Moducciani handbag and it was in your hands three days later. Perfume, jewellery, clothes. He gave you everything. And, it turns out, paid for nothing. He'll be out in a few years, but you're not hanging around for him.

What ties all three of them together? It's where you picked them up. You met all three of them at the Dog and Duck, the only pub in town that has metal grilles on the windows.

You LIKE The Dog and Duck, don't you? You've been going for YEARS, haven't you? They know you by name, and, yes, everyone's a bit rough at the edges, but they've all got heart. These folk are friends for life. If only you could find the right man in the midst of them.

You can't. You won't. You are fucked if you keep trying.

This is how you find the person you're going to share your life with:

1. IDENTIFY YOUR TARGET.

Put some thought into this and focus on QUALITIES, not circumstances.

For example: '*My perfect woman has big tits and a short skirt*' is perfectly admirable if you're a tosser, but the tits will go south and the skirt will be removed (wahey!) and replaced with dungarees or something (boo!).

So try instead: '*My perfect woman is naturally curious, has a fondness for animals and a sense of humour.*' Of course, all of these could change, but they're less ephemeral than the boobs and the outfit.

Now go a bit further. What do they do for a living? What are they interested in?

You're not going to score a perfect hit, unless you're really lucky, but having an idea of where you're going will really help you get there.

2. SCOPE YOUR HUNTING GROUND.

You will not find your perfect man at the Dog and Duck, unless you're looking for Lenny 'Hard' McHard, Johnny Nonchalant or Steve the Fence.

If your ideal man speaks Japanese, go to Japan. If your ideal woman is a bit porky, get to a Weight Watchers meeting. If he plays polo, learn to ride a horse. If she writes poetry, sit in a posh coffee shop at two o'clock in the afternoon.

Have you seen that film with Hugh Grant where he pretends to be a single dad to get single mums? What further proof do you need that this technique works?

Or that French film with Gerard Depardieu where he and his mate hang around the gates of a woman's prison, figuring that, after a few years inside, ex-detainees might be up for a shag. Well thought out, that.

3. START A CONVERSATION.

Refer back to the chapter on talking to strangers.

And finally, FOLLOW UP.

BANG! You're dating! Before you know it, you're with Mister Right or Little Miss Perfect.

You'll never be entirely sure that it's time to get married. You might be, like, 70 per cent sure. But 70 per cent is enough. Don't waste energy worrying.

You don't *have* to get married. But if one of you wants to and the other has no objections, then do it. It makes you feel good. And that's what you want, right?

RELATIONSHIPS LESSON 6:
HOW TO BE MARRIED

YOUR DATING HAS gone well. So well you've found a keeper and got married. And when you're just married, the sex is great. It's better than sex.

But rocking the bedroom love-boat gets tougher with time. Once you're married and you've been together a few years, getting your kit off and your game on becomes a little trickier.

Here's how you remedy it:

My dear married friend. You know that thing you do where you get home, exhausted after a day of shuffling Very Important Documents for Very Important Clients? The kind of day when your boss has been bellowing halitotic insults in your direction every three minutes and you entertain sadistic fantasies of refashioning his face with a stapler?

The thing you do when you've been on your feet since six in

the morning, your car's blown a tyre and you've spent three of the last four hours cleaning up cat sick?

You know, *that thing*.

The thing where you sack off a proper dinner and you and your wife stick a plastic carton of chicken jalfrezi in the microwave, open a bottle of Chablis and collapse in front of the TV?

GREAT, isn't it?

The. Best. Thing. Ever.

Your day's burdens drift effortlessly away as you fill your stomach with Delhi's finest foodstuffs and your mind switches from 'on' to 'off' in the time it takes Eva Longoria to stroll minxily down the stairs in her claret negligée.

Bliss.

But you know that other thing? The elephant-in-the-room-thing?[32] The one that you don't talk about for fear of making it worse? The one where you…

… HAVEN'T HAD SEX WITH YOUR WIFE FOR MONTHS?

Yep. Thought so.

THE TWO ARE CONNECTED. If you spend the evenings mindlessly shovelling food into your gormless gob, you will have less sex.

You say:

---

[32] This is the second elephant-related metaphor in this book. Unfortunately, due to a bout of sloppy editing, this metaphor was explained in a previous footnote.

'Sure, but but but, it's nothing to do with our eating habits. The bedroom and the kitchen aren't connected. The most sex we've ever had was on our honeymoon and THAT'S NORMAL. We don't even want to have more sex. We're TIRED come the close of the day. No energy. We work hard. Sure, we might collapse in front of the idiot-box, but, even if we didn't, we wouldn't be actually, you know, sleeping with each other. That's for teenagers.'

I say:

'Whatever.'

So this is how you have more sex:

Irrespective of your shitty day, of the bollockings you've got about missed deadlines and not bringing in more clients, irrespective of the size of your tax bill and weight of your kids, do this:

Turn your chicken jalfrezi out of its packaging, stick it on a plate, and set the table for two.

EAT AT THE DINNER TABLE.

Have a conversation.

Don't fall asleep with your plate on your lap (much easier if you're eating at a table).

Retire to the bedroom after a scintillating and thoughtful conversation that reminds you why you're married in the first place.

Initiate some sweet loving and annoy the neighbours with your amorous yelps.

No Nookie = Vicious Circle = No Nookie.

Alternatively, keep eating semi-prostrate and enjoy a barren future, a widening posterior, chronic constipation and diverticulitis. Oh, and no sex.

EAT MEALS SITTING AT THE DINNER TABLE AND HAVE MORE SEX.

YOU WILL THANK ME FOR THIS.

RELATIONSHIPS LESSON 7:
ON RAISING KIDS

YOU DON'T CHOOSE your family. You certainly don't choose your parents. They're either a boon to celebrate or a burden to bear, depending on the numbers on your lottery ticket.

You do, however, choose to have kids. At least, if you're the kind of person that invests in self-help books, it's likely that you chose to have kids. And if you didn't or you haven't had kids, that's OK as well. Let's celebrate diversity. Woo-hoo.

It's difficult to have kids, unless you're not planning them, then they just happen. But it's even more difficult to raise them. Raising kids is *fucking* difficult. Take some solace that there's no right or wrong way of doing it. Kids have been around for squillions of years: much longer than child-rearing manuals.

Child-rearing manuals *can* be useful, so long as they're not didactic. What all new parents want is a child-rearing manual that says:

- Some kids cry.
- Some parents find it difficult.
- Have a drink.
- But only one or you'll regret it when you're up at three in the morning.

I don't know how to raise kids. I improvise furiously. Men are largely useless in this regard[33]. I do, however, have the following observations.

- You will become your parents. You've noticed it already. This means that *your kids* will become very much like you. If this worries you, change the bits about yourself you don't like.
- Kill your kids with kindness. You have a duty to love. And to clothe. You don't have a duty to offer horse-riding lessons and ballet classes if it's beyond your means. Nothing makes you feel less certain of your abilities than competitive child-rearing. But if you're good at cuddles, do that. If you're not, learn.
- If you can't keep yourself out of trouble, don't expect the same of your kids. If you can't get to work on time, why should they get to school on time? If you can't drag yourself away from

[33] Do you see how I have cunningly justified my being a rather useless dad by making a sweeping and absolute statement about the child-rearing abilities of all men? Brilliant! And now it's in writing, so it must be true, no?

Saturday-night TV, don't expect their eyes to be any shape but square. If you live on crisps and cake, don't be surprised if they're fat.

- Your kids did not ask to be born. You may never use the words, 'After all we've done for you.' If you now view your children as an insurance policy for your own old age, then you are a callous fuck.

- Your family comes first. But not to the detriment of your sanity. Take five minutes off. And, once your kids are old enough to look after themselves, let them look after themselves.

RELATIONSHIPS LESSON 8:
EMERGENCY!

YOU'VE READ THIS far about relationships and you're scared that none of it applies to you.

You're scared because you've not found the right partner. Your womb is starting to grow cobwebs and you're convinced that you're destined to spend the rest of your years with only cats for company.

Don't despair!

You've got two possible solutions.

Firstly, if you've got no husband or kids, you can travel ANYWHERE you want, ANY TIME and never have to justify your latest Balenciaga purchase. Imagine all the sex you can have! Imagine all the rum you can drink! Imagine how disgracefully you can behave with nobody to say, 'Mum! You're embarrassing me!'

So choice one is to grow old disgracefully and have as much irresponsible fun as you can pack in to your golden years.

And while that first option might appeal to a few of you, it will take an almighty change of mind-set to convince yourself that you're better off alone if you've already decided that you want company.

What you will prefer in this instance is the opportunity to share your life with some special people. But you don't know where to find them.

So buy them.

I'm deadly serious. Your second option is to buy your family, specifically, buy some kids.

Ask any mother whether she'd give precedence to her kids or her husband if the house was burning down. She will always save the kids. That's because kids are *better*. So, once you're sure that nature's not going to play nicely and give you the sprogs you need, start to play Mother Nature yourself. She doesn't exist, so she won't mind.

If you're uncomfortable with this idea, you need to shed your received notions about what's right and proper and what's done and what's acceptable and start to celebrate both medical science and opportunities for loving that are created from occasional misfortune.

As a single woman hell-bent on starting a family but without a man to help you, you've got a myriad of choices. Freeze your eggs, source some sperm (I think you can buy it on the internet now, although I'm not sure that's a great idea). If that doesn't work for you, adopt.

Adoption is for ever. Adoption saves lives. Giving a home to a child is the greatest legacy you can leave behind.

BUT MAKE SURE THAT'S WHAT YOU WANT.

If what you *really* want is a man, then refer back to the section on dating.

And get a bloody move on.

PART FIVE

HEALTH

THIS CHAPTER IS going to be mercifully short. It's about you and your health and is yet another example of me repeating stuff to you that you already know, but prefer to ignore.

Your health equals a large part of your happiness. You hear it all the time and you understand it's true because you're not an idiot. Well, perhaps you are, but you had the good sense to pick up this book, so there's a smidgen of smarts in you somewhere.

Without your health, your happiness is compromised. You might be some kind of saint that can grit your teeth as you pass kidney stones, pondering beatifically on the great mercies bestowed upon humankind by the Good Lord Himself, but it's unlikely. It's infinitely more probable that you can only focus on the sensation of chilli-dipped broken glass passing its way down your urinary tract – a sensation not so conducive to glee, love-making and Irish jiggery.

When it comes to looking after your body, there's nothing new I can tell you. You've already been the recipient of the entire wealth of medical knowledge and experience from every newspaper, men's magazine, women's magazine and chunk of daytime TV you consumed.

The advice changes frequently, admittedly. It can be confusing to be told that tomatoes protect you from bowel cancer, but may exacerbate the symptoms of diverticulitis. Red wine is good AND bad for you depending on the quantity, colour and grape. An aspirin a day lowers the risk of prostate problems, but increases the likelihood of you burning a hole in your stomach lining.

So apply your own rules of common sense.

Most medical advice is generally good. I like to think the world of medical science is competent enough today to avoid recommending remedies that are either highly suspect (fingering women of a 'nervous disposition' to reduce hysteria, anyone?) or downright dangerous (trepanning, for starters[34]).

It's your choice what you do with all the good advice. You can implement it or you can ignore it.

Of course, if you implement it, there is still a risk that you will snuff it before your time. That's life (and death). It is what it is, so don't lose sleep over it.

---

[34] Trepanning is the act of drilling a hole in the skull. It has been used with low levels of success by doctors throughout the ages to relieve the symptoms of epilepsy, migraines and lunacy. It has also been used with greater success as a means of dispensing with awkward patients.

But if you choose to ignore all the good advice you are bombarded with by government departments, newspaper editors and parents, you risk being buried in a reinforced coffin a few months shy of your 50th birthday. Should this happen, the grief and sympathy that your family experience will be tainted with a sense of having been cheated. They will harbour a nagging suspicion that, had you not been such a gluttonous, slothful bastard then you might have been around to pull your weight, wash the dishes and play with your grandkids.

Doctors are there to help. They will give you good advice. There is also a TON of free information available to you, online and offline about the quickest way to burn a verruca (liquid nitrogen), avoid bleach poisoning (don't drink bleach) and expel foreign objects from your anus (various solutions, depending on the size and shape of the inconvenience).

But doctors and medical journals can only tell you what you need to do. The actual *doing* comes down to you, unless it involves anaesthetic, scalpels and removal of aforementioned arse-invaders.

You have the knowledge to start the action. You know how to not get fat, or at least how to get less fat. You know how to boost your levels of dynamism and enjoy energy akin to an amphetamine-fuelled five-year-old. You know all of this and a great deal more. You've just got problems with the execution.

The execution is difficult for two reasons.

1. YOU THINK YOU'RE IMMUNE TO SERIOUS ILLNESS UNTIL IT HAPPENS TO YOU.

Until you get really, scarily, tremblingly, pukingly and malevolently sick, you have this idea that you're a superhero. Perhaps a superhero ostrich with your head shoved so firmly in the sand that the deleterious effects of physical neglect will wander by without noticing you. But you've left your arse sticking out. The deleterious effects of physical neglect will not pass you by, because you are not a superhero.

2. YOU ARE HUMAN.

You suffer the little inconveniences like all of us: lumbago, repetitive strain injury, haemorrhoids and bunions. But you think that the bigger stuff, the cancer, the emphysema, the diabetes, only happen to other people, people who have suffered an unfortunate bout of bad luck.

You know that geezer who had a stroke? Well, it wasn't you, was it? He was unlucky, while you've been lucky. And then there was that old girl who had cirrhosis of the liver after a lifetime of lunchtime Lambrinis? Thank God that wasn't you – but for the grace of God etc – you've got a stronger constitution.

In fact, it never *is* you, not until it is.

'*BUT*,' you say, '*BUT, but let's not focus too much on what MIGHT be and live more in the moment. Life's about enjoyment, right? You said so yourself! We need to focus on what's important and let's face it; it's not really that important for me to pound the 100 metres in under a minute, is it? Athletics is for young people. And who needs to climb stairs without getting out of breath? That's what the lift is for.'*

Look, just, whatever. If that's your take, take your take elsewhere. I can't help you.

This chapter won't save your life. It won't make you healthy, and it won't get you running a marathon.

You KNOW you need to do some exercise, so DO IT. If you're having trouble finding the time, re-read the chapter on getting stuff done. If you're not sufficiently motivated, pay somebody to shout at you so that you leap out of bed and blast out 60 burpees and some crunches before a breakfast of granola and kiwi chips.

And what about the food you eat? It all comes out the same colour, so what does it matter what it looks like when it goes in?

I'm not going to tell you why it matters. You know that it does.

And remedying what you eat is the easiest bit. Just stop eating shit. It will be more difficult if you live in Scotland, but you'll still be able to find something green to eat somewhere.

For that single piece of slightly profane advice, this book has given you an extra few years of your life.

Stop eating shit, live longer and die happy.

I could draw up a table here with Good Food in the left column and Bad Food in the right column, only there's no point, because it's already burned on your memory. Leafy vegetables, fruit and pulses are in the left-hand column.

Saturated fats, refined sugars, too much booze and an over-abundance of shiny fried food is the stuff that's going to kill you, and lives in the right column.

Bad food will kill you by clogging your arteries, festering malignantly in your lower colon, decreasing your metabolic rate and making you lardy. Fat kills.

No surprises there. Yet still you say, '*I know this triple-stuffed-magical-meat-and-triple-cheese deep-pan pizza is bad for me, but I'm only having one. I'll eat a lettuce to balance it out.*'

And you say it every day.

But a lettuce doesn't balance it out. And Diet Coke doesn't cancel out your Five Quarter Pounder Hot Sauce Corndog.

(Plus Diet Coke is sweetened with aspartame. I'm not sure what it is and am therefore afraid of it. At least sugar grows on trees. Kind of.)

Read these chapters briefly. Then eat some sprouts or something. You'll thank me.

HEALTH LESSON 1:
A WORD ON DIET

A FEW WORDS on diet:

This isn't a few words about 'a' diet. I'm not going to recommend living off spinach for four weeks, or cleansing your colon with maple syrup and corn husks. Nor will I suggest giving up carbohydrates and living in an ashram. Diets work for a little while and then they stop working[35].

Diets are useful if you need something to read and only a diet book can scratch the itch. Diets can be a decent quick fix if you're occasionally neurotic, mildly delusional or suffering from irritable bowel syndrome. Diets can be fantastic for having something to talk about when you're having your fingernails waxed or in the waiting for your monthly refill at the Botox clinic.

---

[35] Rather like giving up smoking, which is almost the easiest thing ever. It's not as easy, unfortunately, as taking up smoking again the next day.

If you're interested in diets, food-combining regimes, green smoothies or surviving on nothing but oxygen and filtered rainwater, I can't help you. But there are lots of people who can. I suggest you head to the bookshop. There are currently 2,872,456 (approx) different diets available for you to buy in book form, including diets developed by yoga teachers, firemen, weightlifters, circus dwarves, princesses, disgraced celebrities and doctors of philology.

Some of these diets claim to conquer diabetes, some fight high blood pressure and bad breath, others persuade you that if you 'think' thin you can '*be*' thin, and some are designed to refashion fat ankles, or 'fankles' as they're known in the trade.

There's a diet book out there with your name on it. Seek and ye shall find. But you won't find any diets here I'm afraid and no recipes[36].

But let's talk about food!

Food is medicine.

- When you've been shat on from a great height by your philandering husband, there is no cure like a gaggle of girlies, a box of sushi and two boxes of chocolates, three bottles of vodka and a voodoo doll.

---

[36] Oh all right then, just one. Here's the perfect Bloody Mary: mix one part premium vodka to three parts tomato juice. Add salt, pepper, Worcestershire sauce, Tabasco sauce to taste, and top with a large teaspoon of horseradish. Pour over ice, and stir. Garnish with a stick of celery. Do not eat the celery. It will waste valuable calories.

- When you've woken up with the mother of all hangovers, a bacon sandwich, a large cup of sugary tea and hot bath will restore your electrolytes, rebalance your essential fluids and ease your sore head. It won't help you remember anything you did beyond 11 o'clock, though.
- Discomfort caused by piles can be alleviated by substituting a chicken korma for a mutton vindaloo.

Food is a gateway to goodness.

- Oysters and champagne are a precursor to adventurous sex.
- Roast turkey and mince pies are the harbinger of a joyous family occasion. At least for half an hour, after which there may be more angst than joy, but you can blame Uncle Joe for that one. He always manages to fuck everything up.
- Strawberries and cream ring in the beginning of Wimbledon. Time to leave the country for two weeks.

Food is identity.

- If you are a follower of Judaism or Islam, you eschew the meat of the swine. If you are Buddhist, you strive for vegetarianism.
- If you care about the environment and the suffering of other living beings, and battle ferociously and energetically against the iniquities and atrocities perpetuated against the

natural and the animal world, you eat organic vegetarian sustainable sprouting greens and hemp pancakes.

- If you don't give a shit, you eat anything with great vim and gusto.

Yes, food can be a truly marvellous thing.

But food has a dark side, a dark side you ignore at your peril.

FOOD KILLS.

Yes – you read that right. Food kills. Any edible substance, ingested in the wrong quantity, will cause you to die down dead.

And I'm not just talking about dubious-looking mushrooms or exotic fish that need dissecting by a surgeon or out-of-date seared tripe that's been left in the sun for three weeks. I'm talking about EVERYTHING.

Admittedly, some stuff's more toxic than the rest. But even acai berries, seaweed, battered cod, California sun-dried raisins and peanut butter on toast will cause the death of you if you eat too much of the stuff.

Even water, when over-done, will push you over the edge. If you don't believe me, try drinking 11 litres of water in the next 15 minutes[37].

In sufficient quantity, everything is a poison and, if you eat or drink too much of anything, you will die.

[37] VERY IMPORTANT: DO NOT DO THIS. I REPEAT, DO NOT DO THIS. You will die and the author and publishers and whoever sold you this book will not be held liable for disposal of your body or any associated costs or reparations.

YOU DO NOT HAVE TO CLEAR YOUR PLATE.

Generosity and obligation are behind big portions. The host feels magnanimous by overloading your plate and you feel obliged to finish everything on it.

YOU DO NOT HAVE TO FINISH EVERYTHING.

Slow down a little and stop when you're full. It's your body.

Unless you're Jock 'Fatty' McFat, you're unlikely to ever be in the situation where you consume SO much of one substance that it puts you 10 feet under before you've had time to wipe your mouth.

So (and here's the big point):

Eat whatever you like and drink whatever you like and, while remembering that you will certainly die of something, don't be the dick that kicks the bucket from an overdose of smoked salmon and cream cheese.

HEALTH LESSON 2:
YOUR BODY

YOU'RE NOT HAPPY with your body, you say? Boo fucking hoo. You were born with your body, so live with it. It's non-negotiable.

What's the matter? You've got big ears? Pigeon toes? A fat arse? Distended labia?

So you don't look like Errol Flynn or Audrey Hepburn? Join the club. And get over it.

You don't choose your body; it's the vehicle that carries your brilliant grey cells and furious intellect through life. Since birth it's changed a bit and it will change a bit more over the next few months and years. By the time you're minutes from death, wheezing on your oxygen machine, you'll barely be recognisable.

You can control some of these physical changes, but not all of them.

If you've been reading this book properly, perhaps you've already danced naked in front of the mirror, as previously directed?

Maybe you even dance naked on a regular basis as part of your daily routine? If so, be sure to video yourself next time and email it to me[38].

But chances are you only *thought* about dancing naked, but were having such fun reading this rollicking rollercoaster of a book that you skipped happily on to the next chapter, hoping that by reading and not doing you'll get the same results.

(You won't.)

Consequently, you still have at least one serious issue with your body. And you can't do anything about it, other than stop worrying about it.

That's because your skin and your morphology (that's your 'body type') are things that can only be tackled by a plastic surgeon. While cosmetic surgery is a wonderful advancement of science and proof of the ability of mankind to mess with all kinds of shit that we should really leave alone, the results are a bit *weird*. The resulting perky tits, surprised eyes and expressionless, balloon-like lips are not traits to aspire to. They are traits to run from.

Your body is yours alone. Live with it.

Take your big nose, for example. It's huge and unattractive, isn't it?

---

[38] AGAIN, DO NOT DO THIS. THIS IS A JOKE. I DO NOT WANT YOU TO SEND ME NAKED VIDEOS OF YOURSELF. Any videos received of readers dancing in the nude will not be viewed, but sold immediately to Dirty Ken, who has a DVD stall at Brixton market.

NO it's NOT! Get a grip! What's your nose too big for? Smelling stuff? And don't start on about your hips again. Your hips are too big? Are you SERIOUS? Too big for what? Holding your legs in place?

I mean, *seriously.*

Since when did a big nose stop you doing anything you wanted to do? Were you so set on being a nose model that your life plans have been dashed because of your oversized conk? Do nose models even exist?

Your big nose wasn't responsible for you not doing stuff you would have quite liked to do. *Your idea* that your nose was too big to do stuff was what stopped you from doing stuff.

Would you like to have a candlelit dinner with Deborah from mergers and acquisitions? '*Oh no, I couldn't possibly, my nose is far too big and she'd find me deeply lacking in humanity, wit and charm.*'

Loser.

And, madam, what about your wonderful womanly hips? Those curvaceous, feminine, enviable and lust-worthy saddlebags that you hide from the world?

'*I couldn't possibly stand up in front of Jason, even though I've had my eye on him since he started delivering the mail six months ago. He's gorgeous, but, if I stood up, he'd see how wide my flanks are and never talk to me again!*'

(Incidentally, if that *is* Jason's response, Jason's a fucking tool and you should hook up with Frank who's been eyeing you up for the last eight months but is too shy to say hello.)

Ah yes, but Frank has sticking-out ears.

JESUS, PEOPLE! GET OVER IT!

You are born with your body, much the same as every other ugly bastard was born with theirs. The sooner you start to either love it or become indifferent to it, the sooner you'll start to enjoy life a little more.

Yes, if you're a bit fat, there's something you can try to do about it. Start with emptying the fridge of cream cakes. If your fingers are nicotine-stained, invest in a mother-of-pearl cigarette holder. If your beard is ginger, shave it off.

But if you're a bit short, you're a bit short. Find somebody with a midget fetish and enjoy the best sex of your life.

There are some people you're meant to sleep with and there are some that you are not. Similarly, there are some people you're meant to be friends with and there are some that you are meant to avoid. Do yourself a favour and concentrate on finding the former. These people do not care what you look like.

At this stage, another book or article might tell you to stop reading magazines that reinforce the 'body perfect'. Another article might tell you to leave the homo-erotic magazines about men's health issues on the newsstand and eschew magazines with exclamation marks in their titles that tell you how to get a Hollywood smile with some bicarbonate of soda and a little elbow grease.

But I'm not going to tell you that. I like to look at pictures of semi-naked people. They are eye-food.

Adopt the same attitude to the body perfect as you do professional footballers with drug problems: 'They are good; therefore I am deriving some enjoyment from watching them. But I am very glad that I am me, because I am much better off.'

You have to live with your body. So make peace with it. Or forever fight a losing battle.

HEALTH LESSON 3:
GET SOME SLEEP!

SLEEP IS GOOD for you. So what's your excuse? You're dozing at your desk, drifting through the delicatessen with your eyes half-shut and watching life go by as if from the window of a train.

For God's sake, man, GET SOME SLEEP!

What are you doing collapsed on the sofa, biscuit crumbs in your lap, semi-consciously channel-surfing in the hope that you don't 'miss anything'?

Your wife nudges you and says, 'Stop snoring,' and you respond, 'I'm not asleep!'

What are you? Six? You want to stay up late because it's cool? RUBBISH! GET YOUR REST!

The benefits of sleep:

- The ability to safely operate heavy machinery, such as tractors, industrial printing presses and wind-turbines, without endangering the lives of you and your fellow workers.

- Clear-headed decision-making, protecting you from the cunning wiles of timeshare salesmen, insurance agents and boiler-room penny-stock vendors who call you at home with an 'exclusive' opportunity that's only available for the next 15 minutes.
- Glowing skin that will get you noticed by talent-scouts and have you on the front-page of glossy magazines, drinking champagne cocktails and snorting coke off platinum trays.
- The only opportunity you'll ever get to legitimately cheat on your wife with Eva Longoria, albeit in a dream.

So, it's late, you're tired. Here are your choices:

1. Stay where you are, watch a series of semi-clad women pretend to talk to you on the phone while performing surprisingly repetitive stand-up, sit-down, take-off-shirt actions, then switch to watch a bearded man subtitled by a sign-language interpreter instruct you on the atomic make-up of a rock, before catching the tail-end of an eastern European film set in an industrial estate.
2. Go to bed.

Option 1 = waking up at three o'clock in the morning with a stiff neck, dribble all over your chin, fully clothed and wide awake.

You crawl to bed, neglect your personal hygiene and wake up three hours later in the middle of a sleep cycle. You suck.

Option 2 = THE WIN! You wake up early like an eager bunny and grasp the day by the bollocks.

GO TO BED = YOU WON'T MISS A THING = WORLD DOMINATION

TOP SECRET EXTRA INFORMATION

If you go to bed early, and get up early, you'll have more hours in the day and you'll be a step closer to superstardom.

But the real key to superstardom is to sleep IN THE MIDDLE OF THE DAY.

There is NOTHING that can't wait 45 minutes while you shut your eyes and drift off immediately after lunch.

Close the curtains, take off your socks, set your alarm clock and revel in the blissful and slightly naughty sensation of being asleep when everybody else is awake.

The siesta is the quickest route to long life. This is official.

HEALTH LESSON 4:

EAT BREAKFAST

YOU'VE WOKEN UP after a good night's sleep. Brilliant! Now it's time for breakfast. Breakfast rocks. You don't eat breakfast, you fail. Breakfast is the breakfast of champions.

YOU DON'T NEED REMINDING OF THIS.

There's a story in every newspaper at least once a month, telling you that breakfast is the cornerstone of weight loss, productivity and general all-round awesomeness. Breakfast will give you more energy, a metabolism boost and Marmite-coated crumbs you can pick out of your beard when you get hungry later in the day.

Breakfast-junkies the world over expound on their awesome morning routines which involve getting up at half past two, meditating, working for eight hours, fixing global warming and stopping wars before a high-energy, low-carb, protein-rich breakfast.

But you don't. You miss it. A coffee and a cigarette is the best you manage and you feel seriously sucky come 11 o'clock.

You NEED breakfast because if you don't have it:

- Your stomach rumbles all the way through your morning meetings and the sexy guy from marketing keeps his distance.
- Your breath smells.
- You're an irritable bastard, losing the love and respect of friends with each minute that passes.
- You're lethargic and slovenly, your work suffers and you lose your job.

NO BREAKFAST = UNEMPLOYMENT and LONELINESS.

With breakfast in your life, you have more energy for your work and your friends, the ability to sustain longer lovemaking sessions and better breath.

You rock.

YOU DON'T EAT BREAKFAST BECAUSE:

- You don't have time
- You don't have time
- You get up too late
- You don't have time

You say:

'*Hang on a second, I don't eat breakfast because I'm not a morning eater. I really don't get hungry until about the middle of the morning.*'

I CALL BULLSHIT!

You know when you go on holiday or you're away on a business trip and staying in a lush hotel that serves just about everything you could want to eat? You know those times? You know how you ALWAYS manage to eat breakfast in those situations?

Yeah, thought so.

But working on the assumption that you don't have a man to iron your newspaper, press your slacks and polish your spats before serving up half a pound of kedgeree prepared according to his great-grandmother's secret recipe, you've got to deal with breakfast yourself.

The good news is, it's bloody easy. You can prepare your own morning meal in less than 10 seconds. Here's how:

- Open cereal, empty into previously prepared empty bowl.
- Pour on milk from previously prepared milk container.
- Eat.

OR

- Open oatmeal (porridge where I come from), pour into bowl.

- Pour on hot water, leave to stand.
- Eat.

BANG! INSTANT BREAKFAST!

Don't let the power of being able to make breakfast imbue you with a misplaced sensation of culinary courage. It will be a while before the BBC is banging down your door to make a cookery show. Once you graduate to baked beans on toast, however, you might want to get an agent.

HEALTH LESSON 5:
DRINK MORE WATER

SO, YOU'RE NO longer eating too much rubbish, breakfast is part of your morning routine, you've had a great night's sleep and you leave an appreciative little lump of uneaten food on your plate.

You're getting there, but you probably don't drink enough water[39].

You're probably a little dehydrated and it's making you slow and heavy.

Water is good for you. Water keeps your brain thinking and your lungs breathing and your stomach digesting and your spleen doing whatever it is that spleens do.

So, my friend, drink more water.

---

[39] You might remember that water can kill you. Water WILL kill you if you have too much of it too quickly. Exercise discretion.

Get a large glass, fill it to the brim with the wonderful clear liquid that is the lifestuff of, er, life, and pour it down your parched gullet.

Feels good, doesn't it?

Do it again.

And then take a break until you're thirsty.

(It is said, by folk wiser than me, that once you're thirsty it's already TOO LATE. But I think that's a scare we can afford to discount for now, for want of overloading our already tired brains with too much information.)

If you're prone to hyperhydrosis (you sweat a lot), you might need more water than others. If you live in the Mediterranean and the days are warm and sticky, you'll need to drink more than if you're holed up in a semi-detached in Kingston-Upon-Thames.

What's certain, my shrivelled little reader, is that you're not getting your recommended daily allowance of dihydrogen monoxide.

But it's such a hassle, isn't it, drinking water? You have to remember to do it, for a start.

It's much easier to crack open a can of fizzy pop than find a glass, find a tap, execute effective opening of the tap, stop the tap and start to drink.

But seriously, fizzy drinks? Would you shower in them? Would you even wash your car with them? Of course you wouldn't. But it doesn't stop you pouring the sticky carbonated juices *inside* your body on a daily basis.

Water, thankfully, has come back into fashion of late. The

magical marketing men at the soft drink giants have realised they can command enormous mark-up levels on good old-fashioned water. They have done, therefore, a damn fine job of showing us how we can top ourselves up with our preferred brand of cloud liquid while on the go.

This is why you see folk walking around with bottles of water glued to their hands. This was unheard of 20 years ago; only paramedics and professional athletes and catering professionals needed water wherever they went. But this is PROGRESS, I hear! You can't be without your bottle today, or you'll feel bare!

You can even buy jewel-encrusted bottles that are promoted by vacuous celebrities. Just imagine that! There are hotels and restaurants that have water concierges, in case you're uncertain about which brand might best suit your physiology or some such nonsense.

This is, of course, testament to idiocy. If you're lucky enough to be reading this book in a place where good drinking water comes out of your tap, then water is basically free.

If you're one of those unfortunate sods whose lot in life means that they have to trek cross-country on a daily basis to get dirty drinking water for you and the rest of your extended family, then might I suggest that reading this book isn't the best investment of your time? (And I seriously hope you haven't spent your own hard-earned money on buying this.)

So here's your action plan, because you ignored my suggestion earlier on.

Read to the end of this chapter.

Get up out of your overstuffed armchair and walk to the kitchen.

Pour yourself a glass of water.

Repeat every now and again.

YOU ROCK! You've just solved half your health problems in one fell swoop![40]

Your pee should be a very light-yellow colour. If you find the prospect of inspecting the colour of your pee distasteful, please repeat the chapter on taking yourself less seriously.

---

[40] You may not, actually, have solved half your health problems in one fell swoop. This is, in fact, a wildly exaggerated and fallacious claim, made by an individual with no background in medicine or alternative health. No responsibility will be taken by the author or publishers of this book should you decide to stop taking any course of medication you may now be following as a direct result of the claim made on the last page of this chapter.

HEALTH LESSON 6:
IN DEFENCE OF BOOZE

BOOZE. DON'T YOU love it?

Is there anything, *anything* more rewarding than an ice-cold beer at the end of a day spent toiling in the fields or breaking rocks by the side of the highway or sweeping the streets of ragged anti-government protestors?

Can you think of a more stylish start to a weekend than drinking a resplendent red Bloody Mary, decorated with a crisp green stalk of celery and a plate of eggs Benedict on the side[41]? And as Jeeves is buttering your toast and asking if sir wouldn't like another coffee, you say, '*Well, it would be a shame to waste the rest of the tomato juice. Top me up with another Bloody Mary, there's a good man.*'

Civilisation wouldn't be nearly as civilised without pre-

[41] See the beginning of this section for a world-beating Bloody Mary recipe.

prandial vodka martinis and post-prandial brandies. Wars have been won in drawing rooms of country manors by pissed old generals in a fug of port and cigar smoke.

Children have been born of booze. Liquor gave the young lovemaking participants a sense of daring and romance that they lacked sober. And thus they had babies. Often these children weren't planned for, admittedly. But would any of you with a wee bairn who appeared as a result of too many margaritas and a free hotel room like to trade in your nippers for a new car or a pair of jeans? Of course not.

Alcohol is a creative lubricant. It fuels writers and poets and artists. As I sit at my typewriter this afternoon, I am happily pissed and consequently entirely convinced of my lucidity, alacrity and wit. I am brilliant and you, lucky reader, are riding pillion on this slightly tipsy journey of wonder. Be gentle with me, should I start to repeat myself.

Booze is the social destuckifier of choice for wallflowers and shy-guys the world over. Is there anything more terrifying than entering a party where you don't know a soul? You end up being forced to make polite conversation with the wife of the host's business partner, who doesn't really want to be there either, but is the only person not having fun. So you cling to each other all night, making stilted small talk and humming and rattling your glasses through the long silences.

But head straight for the bar, sink three Slippery Nipples and you'll find that the party *comes to you*. Before the end of the night you'll be necking the barmaid and booked on a flight to Vegas that leaves in a few hours.

And a couple of whiskys[42] are the perfect solution to many of life's tricky issues. In fact, the gravity of any given problem is inversely proportional to the hour of the day and the number of shots you've had. At three in the morning, waking up in the middle of the night sweaty with the terrors, you feel that you've got an insurmountable issue on your hands. But as the day goes on, your problem becomes less scary. And at nine in the evening, after four single malts and a plate of meatballs, you haven't even got an inkling of a problem.

Yes, booze is a wonderful thing, when you're the boss.

But if you're teetering on the brink of losing boss-dom over the bottle, it's time to take action.

You need to know when to crack the whip. The demons that live in the dregs of your Drambuie bottle need to be told that they're not coming out to play tonight because you have to work in the morning or you're on the verge of losing your wife.

If you've had to take more than three days off work in the last year because of a crippling hangover, then you have a problem. It's time to take responsibility for yourself.

---

[42] Spelling of whisky here is deliberate and quite correct. If your brand is commonly served with a soft drink mixer, it's not spelled like this, and that's fine, because it's a different drink.

The advice that follows in the next chapter is not for you if you are an alcoholic or you think you may be an alcoholic[43].

---

[43] Incidentally, if you think you're an alcoholic, you probably are. If you think you might be fighting a losing battle with drink, then you just may be. Either that, or you're prone to hysteria. In any case, it's a good idea to get help.

HEALTH LESSON 7:
TRY HOMEOPATHIC DRINKING

SO HERE'S HOW to get a grip on booze, courtesy of the world of homeopathy.

For those of you unfamiliar with homeopathy, it's a sort of medicinal science that suggests that the best quantity of the substance you need to tackle your ills is basically none at all.

In fact, the mere *memory* of whatever it is you need to take to get better is enough to get you better.

For example, a homeopathic concoction designed to cure your gout might include one part of active gout remedy – for example, a desiccated badger's foreskin – to one million parts water.

Now is not the time to debate whether or not homeopathy works. It does or it doesn't, depending on your informed and educated opinion.

Now is, however, the time to apply the principles of homeopathy to a decent boozing session, to leave you potent in the bedroom and clear-headed in the morning.

The fabulously wealthy lushes who flock to the French Riviera each summer to bare their bronzed chests on boats filled with rappers and girls with big boobs have known this particular trick for years. It's the application of the homeopathic drinking technique that lets them spend 10 days in a slightly tipsy fug of white wine and bubbles.

They mix their wine with water.

And that's the trick.

'*BUT THAT'S SACRILEGE!*' you say, enraged that the grape should be besmirched by the addition of common-or-garden tap juice.

But it works. You can make a bottle of wine last a whole day if you dilute it liberally with six bottles of *eau pétillante.*

And if the biblical idea of wine and water doesn't gel with you, try this:

On your next visit to Mushi Mushi's Nightclub, order yourself one gin and tonic. Before you've finished it, order yourself another tonic. Before you've finished that one, order a tonic again.

Keep the same glass all night. Don't add any more gin. The mere *memory* of the gin will work its wonders and you'll wake up fresh-headed and resistant to malaria.

HEALTH LESSON 8:
EMBRACE YOUR HANGOVER

IF YOU IGNORE the advice from the last chapter, you're going to wake up with a hangover. The main problem with hangovers isn't the physical side. The sore head and the niggling nausea can be attacked with various food-based remedies.

The REAL problem with hangovers is the insistent knock-knocking of non-specific guilt, guilt about having offended somebody or having made a dick of yourself.

But also (and this is the bit to drop RIGHT NOW), guilt about being 'unproductive' and useless as you potter about feeling like your digestive system is inverted.

YOU took a decision to get drunk, to dance the conga and, most likely, to enjoy yourself.

NOW take a decision to indulge your hangover. This is the price to pay for a good night on the sauce.

DO NOT COMPLAIN. DO NOT MOAN.

YING/YANG, ACTION/REACTION, DRUNK/HUNGOVER.

The world won't stop if you put on a weepy film, eat ice-cream and drink lemonade all day long. Give yourself permission to have a day off. Guilt will eat at you, given a chance, so tackle it head-on.

You welcomed your hangover in, so you take responsibility for its wellbeing. Greet it with a vigorous nod, pop a couple of aspirin and quit beating yourself up[44].

---

[44] Disclaimer – and a repetition of the previous disclaimer – if you're over 25 and experiencing hangovers more than two or three times a week, ignore this advice and get some real help. You need it.

PART SIX

WORK AND MONEY

ARRGH! DESPITE ALL the cool stuff we've been talking about – the health, happiness, relationships and stuff – work and money always seem to get in the way. Despite your best efforts, this is where most of your time and emotional energy seems to go, isn't it?

However many times you say to yourself, '*Must focus on health and happiness and relationships and the nice fuzzy feelings that multiply in your solar plexus when all the soft, right-brain side of my life is going well*', you still end up having to get in the car or on the bus each morning and slope off to the daily grind of work.

You have to work because you need the cash to live.

You need the cash to live because you're a responsible adult, and this a good thing[45].

---

[45] If you've decided that you're not going to get up and go to work for your cash, but prefer to rely on the handouts of the state or of parents or of elderly and mentally infirm relatives, then good for you. You won't need this chapter, you indolent, scrounging, good-for-nothing.

If only it didn't SUCK SO MUCH.

Work sucks. And most money issues suck. Paying off credit-card debt sucks. Paying taxes sucks, especially when you see them being spent on the housing and rehabilitation of the foul-mouthed chav who nicked your video recorder last Christmas.

But, if you need money, you've got to work. Live with it.

This chapter deals with making work suck less and repeating some of the oft-quoted and even more often ignored advice on cash, and debt, and stuff.

WORK AND MONEY LESSON 1:
YOUR JOB IS WHAT YOU DO, NOT WHO YOU ARE

WORK SUCKS, INNIT?

In fact, you might be lucky. Your job might not be mind-blowing, but it could be 'OK' or 'not too bad'. More likely, however, it's just plain 'terrible'.

You went to school; you passed all your exams, you graduated through college and a series of demeaning jobs before landing the professional gig you always wanted to do. And now you've been doing it without too much enthusiasm for the last six years.

So this is important advice.

In a moment, I'll show you how to go from subservient doormat, permanently cowering at the sound of the boss's footsteps, to being Chief Executive of The Awesome Corporation.

But you're not there yet, so in the meantime you have to learn and repeat this mantra[46].

(Drum roll please…)

'My job is what I do, not who I am.'

If your job involves digging holes or stuffing sandwiches or licking staples, it doesn't mean you're a hole-digger, sandwich-stuffer or staple-licker. That's just what you do at work.

If you're a lawyer, folk will presume you're the money-grabbing, duplicitous, meretricious spawn of Satan. But they'd be wrong, wouldn't they? You just happen to practise law.

People who are worth your while will not judge you for being brilliant at the stuff you do between nine and five. People who are worth your while will not even care what it is you do for a living (unless you work in tobacco or firearms marketing).

You will not be judged by people who are worth your while for being brilliant at sorting the staples, mastering the photocopier or licking envelopes fast.

And if you're shit at your job? If you've never quite mastered the widgets that make the factory run or you never get employee of the month, don't worry. It doesn't matter.

All the nonsense that happens at the office or the factory

---

[46] I swear that this is the only mantra you'll find in the whole book. I prefer to think of it more as an exhortation or a commandment than a mantra. But if you've been reading up until now and thinking, *'Gosh, this is all very well, but I sure wish I had something I could print off and sellotape to my bathroom mirror to remind myself of something every morning'*, then this is it.

or the wildlife park is what you have to put up with. It's part of the deal.

There may be people who choose to hang out with you because you're an awesome accountant or a kick-ass bootlicker or a mean typist. But these are the kinds of people you'll want to avoid. These same people will say, '*I couldn't possibly hang out with Deborah. Her last presentation on vertical market segmentation totally sucked.*'

The type of person you'll want to hang out with will say, '*I'd love to hang out with Deborah. She's cool. I don't even know what she does for a living.*'

Your friends will be your friends irrespective of your ability to close the deal or flip the burger or answer the phone with a smile.

Sure, it's a bonus if you get to do what you like to do for a living, but you probably don't.

You're in good company.

You can choose to quit your shitty job (more details to follow) or you can choose to live with it. Either way, it's your choice.

If you DO decide to stick with it, bear this in mind:

We are remembered not for the thoughts we had, but for the actions we took. Unless you're the curator of a national institute, politician or other representative of the state, the actions you took at work count for nothing.

Work is what you have to put up with to allow you to do the cool shit.

WORK AND MONEY LESSON 2:
MAKE WORK SUCK LESS

IF WORK IS what you have to put up with, you have to make it suck as little as possible.

The rest of your life is sorted. In fact, you've got everything at home and play down to a sweet shizzle. You're a time-management ninja away from the office. You apply the Eight Minute Rule and outsource to an army of willing Filipinas and teenage gardeners. Home life is finally bearable.

But you've still got to go jump on the bus and head into work every day with a lumpy feeling in your chest.

Those days are long, aren't they? You hate them, really, don't you?

'Don't get me started,' you say. *'Even though I'm the boss I'm wearing this great big fraudulent cape of hypocrisy. I tell all my staff that they should be doing nothing more important than working on next week's sales forecasts or plumping the budgets for*

the annual shareholders' conference or cleaning the widget-maker for the monthly inspection. But in my heart, I'm thinking only of the golf course, next weekend's stag party and my invitation to the Cougars' Ball.'

And if you're not the boss, you have it even worse. You don't have any opportunity for delegation or recursive action when the prospect of stuffing envelopes, oiling machines or sorting through the recyclables leaves you cold. For you, office life truly sucks.

In a couple of chapters' time, I'm going to reveal the single and simple solution to making being in this situation a thing of the past. But, dear student, you're not there yet.

In the meantime, you need some urgent fire-fighting methods to make the working day go faster. Try these and watch the hours fly by.

Firstly, though, here's what NOT to do:

SURF THE INTERNET.

Do not do it. The same rules apply at work as they do at home. If you're lucky enough to work in an office where your computer faces the wall and the IT department doesn't monitor your web-based activity, then the temptation to spend the day poking your ex-boyfriends on Facebook is going to be a strong one.

Maybe somebody has sent you a HILARIOUS video of some dude falling off a skateboard, and when you click through, you see that there are 1900 related videos of other people falling off skateboards.

Watching those videos or trawling through photos of old school friends on Facebook so that you can marvel at how ugly their husbands and kids are is not going to make your day go faster. In fact, mindless surfing of the internet does nothing but make you miserable.

It makes you miserable because you want to feel that you're doing something productive, unless you're on designated downtime. When you're at work, in an environment that *ideally* is one of actual, you know, *work*, then by being specifically unproductive you have buggered up what your day was meant to be about.

(As already mentioned, excessive internet use will also rot your brain. What levels of intelligence you had before you started will slowly be eroded by images of dudes in Bermuda shorts falling off skateboards. Seriously. The capacity of your mind is small enough. Don't fill it with crap.)

The best way to make your work day suck less is:

GOSSIP.

Gossip is what we were put on this earth for. We were NOT put on earth to compile spreadsheets and financial projections. That is a construct of men with clipboards and shiny heads. To communicate with other people is why we are here, so what better use of your time is there than having a real one-to-one conversation with a flesh-and-blood person?

The office is the ULTIMATE place to gossip, because it feels naughty. Because everybody has a label in the modern workplace, you feel that it's inappropriate to talk about the manager, or the CEO, or even the mailroom clerk. That makes it all the more fun.

Gather by the water cooler whenever you can. Talk in whispers. The more inappropriate the subject matter, the better the quality of the gossip.

Two tips for better gossip:

1. Take up smoking, if you don't already. By leaving the office for seven minutes every hour and a half, the opportunities for scandal-mongering present themselves even more frequently[47].

2. If you're going to gossip about others, accept that others will be gossiping about you. Embrace this and be sure that your personal response to hearing rumours about what you got up to at the weekend is dramatic, loud and out of all proportion to the accusations. This will increase the overall level of drama, histrionics and scandal and ensure that the gossip remains juicier for days and weeks to come.

---

[47] Do not take up smoking. My offspring cannot afford the lawsuits that will follow should you take up smoking today and hold me responsible in 40 years' time. Also, do not take up smoking because it is largely understood to be bad for you and may cause you smoking-related diseases.

WORK AND MONEY LESSON 3:
GO ON HOLIDAY

SO YOU'RE AT work, and by the miracle of gossip and cigarette breaks, and the sheer luck of having a boss that doesn't suck, it's not so bad.

Nothing ever gets on top of you.

Every morning you arrive, greet the receptionist with a smile and get down to ticking boxes and adding and subtracting from your to-do list. Your inbox gets to zero, then goes up to 50, then goes down to zero again.

Suppliers are always paid on time because you've got a kick-ass 'how to pay bills' system. You get a gold star from your boss for the last presentation you made on sustainable development in emerging markets and he's mentioned that you might, possibly, be in line for a promotion or, if you're lucky, a special mention at the Christmas party.

The working life for you is OK and you allow yourself to feel a little smug. Keep working hard and by the age of 65 you'll retire and travel the world. The office might even throw you a little party. That's something to look forward to, isn't it?

Isn't it?

No. It's not. It sounds terrible. You have a responsibility to enjoy yourself NOW. Remember, work is what you do from nine-to-five. It is not who you are. It is not how you define yourself. Work, you will recall, is the sucky bit you have to do in order to enjoy the rest of life[48].

So enjoy your life NOW. Do not focus on the riches that will come in retirement by living frugally today. Do not focus on the destination, focus on the journey. And that means taking holidays.

If you're not taking holidays and you're not going abroad, you can add to your bottom line to the tune of a grand or two a year.

What a waste of saved money.

'*Gee, hon, I'm really looking forward to retiring in 25 years. I sure do hope we're alive to see it. We can go holiday. Won't that be fun?*'

NO. No, it won't. It won't be fun. It will be slightly exhausting. Do not save up all your fun-time cash for retirement. Spend it

---

[48] If, in your case, you do live to work, you need to get a life. Work/life balance, for those who can achieve it, is a fine thing. But if you look forward to work more than you look forward to going home at the end of the day, you need to change your home environment. Leave your husband. He's clearly no good for you.

now and have MORE FUN. Climbing Macchu Picchu is bloody difficult at the best of times. Don't make it harder on yourself by waiting for the onset of osteoporosis before you have a go.

Give yourself permission to grab your sandals and bermuda shorts and hit the beach, climb a mountain, eat strange foods in strange places.

Ride a donkey.

Have some fun.

Travel and meet interesting people. If you travel, you get to see stuff and get sick in new places.

Here are a few things to remember in order to make the most of your holidays:

- You will always be a tourist, unless you are a resident. You are not a traveller. You are only allowed to call yourself a traveller if the area you are trekking around has not been mapped, which it has.
- Even if you are a resident in a foreign country, you have not 'gone native' unless you speak the language and marry somebody who was born there. Wearing a sarong is not enough. Nor is the application of henna tattoos and hair-braids.
- By adamantly refusing the sobriquet 'tourist', you risk missing out on the shit that's really worth seeing. You may believe that a trip to Egypt to visit the pyramids is a little cliched. But that's OK. A cliche is a cliche because it is

grounded in truth and sightseeing trips tend to focus on the sights that are really worth seeing. So go on the tourist bus.

- Hanging out with local folk is OK, but not mandatory. It's perfectly legitimate to be a tourist. Hanging out with expat friends is also legitimate. Heading to the Far East and only eating in McDonald's is probably a bit of a dumb idea, all in all. But it's OK. If that's what you want to do, then that's what you want to do.

- People speak different languages in different countries. It's not guaranteed that everybody will be able to communicate in English. If this is likely to be a problem for you, choose a linguistically safe destination like Australia, Canada or Liberia.

- The food is not always the same as you get at home. Sometimes it is spicier, sometimes it is meatier and sometimes it involves the flesh of animals that you do not associate with dinner. If you wish to avoid any culinary surprises, then head to somewhere with food you recognise. The Costa Del Sol, the Canary Islands and Mumbai are good choices.

- The currency used is unlikely to be the same as the currency you have at home. If, for example, you are resident in Great Britain or Northern Ireland, you will find that the only place you are able to spend a sterling penny will be in one of your neighbouring countries. If you live in the Republic of Ireland, you have a little more choice. Almost anywhere in continental Europe has now agreed to accept the Irish euro[49].

---

[49] Incidentally, as an Irish citizen wishing to travel the world, you'll be in excellent company and following in the steps of countless compatriots before you. A happy consequence of the diaspora of Wild Irish Geese is that Guinness can be found anywhere. Be particularly wary, however, of Guinness in a bottle. It is not the same drink.

WORK AND MONEY LESSON 4:
YOUR JOB IS NOT SAFE

SO YOU'RE TAKING your holidays. That's cool. And surprisingly, work's *working out* for you as well.

Look at you, hot property! You've almost got a grip!

It started early in your case, though, didn't it? It started when you were young. You did eight years at medical school with a specialisation in neuro-proctology, four years of training and now YOU ARE THE MAN[50].

You studied hard, young buck, like your mother taught you. You didn't NEED the spankings and the wallopings and the threats of 'making nothing of your life' because you were DRIVEN.

You sweated over homework assignments and you gave up climbing trees with Stacey in order to get your dissertation on the nocturnal micturation habits of the common-or-garden-vole in

[50] Figuratively. You may be a woman.

to the teacher on time. You got a gold star and a smiley face EVERY WEEK.

And in time you graduated and you qualified and you passed your nine-month induction period. Then you toiled, brown-nosed and impressed enough to make partner. And now you are. And you drive a Beemer.

The family holiday in the Bahamas and you get to see them at weekends.

What a rock star.

* * *

Or maybe that wasn't you; perhaps that wasn't your story.

Maybe you didn't find it easy. Maybe you found it really, really tough. You found it tough to concentrate, tough to learn, tough to perform. It's not that you didn't want to do well, it just didn't come naturally.

So you resigned yourself to not making partner, to not being a doctor. You knew your limits and you decided to stick to them.

And so every day you go to work. It doesn't turn you on, tweak your nipples or goose you unexpectedly in the night. It doesn't light up your day and it doesn't light up your eyes.

BUT it's not SO BAD.

In exchange for eight hours de-beaking chickens, ladling gravy, mowing lawns or shining shoes, you get WHAT'S IMPORTANT:

Evenings with your family and food in your kids' mouths.

And that will have to do.

And then this happens:

- Some French dude in a German bank does something he shouldn't on a computer somewhere in Luxembourg and your customers stop spending money. You never even met this guy, but apparently it means you're out of a job.
- The Texan guy with the cigar you only ever see in the parking lot sells something to a minor Saudi royal. Infuriatingly, this means you're no longer needed.
- Your boss elopes with Sharon from audit. He's replaced by Jeremy. Jeremy doesn't like you. You have to go.
- Some fat guy spends your entire pension fund and falls off a boat. You have to go.
- For any number of reasons, all beyond your control, and many beyond your understanding, you have to go.

So you're out of a job. And it's somebody else's fault[51].

But it doesn't have to be that way.

You have another choice:

You can work for yourself.

If you work for yourself you'll never be out of a job and as a bonus you won't have to genuflect and suck up to your boss.

---

[51] This may be one of the opportunities when you don't have to accept responsibility. But responsibility or not, it's still very much YOUR problem.

Sure, you might be short of clients or struggle financially, eat spaghetti hoops for a year or any number of things. But you won't blame somebody else.

You'll have taken the ultimate responsibility for your life.

Scary, huh?

(Don't worry – I'll show you how.)

WORK AND MONEY LESSON 5:
THE TRUTH ABOUT MONEY

YOU'RE ABOUT TO start working for yourself. Time to clear up those money-gremlins that make you go fuzzy headed when you start thinking about finance.

A healthy bank balance and a respectful relationship with money will set you firmly on the path to being the carefree and slightly bohemian cravat-wearing playboy you'd like to be.

Cash can buy you ALL SORTS of nice shit. You can go on holiday to exotic places and get drunk with new people. Your toys can be bigger and more dangerous and more fun. You can skive off work to colour your jowls a deeper crimson or make sizeable and soul-saving contributions to charity to atone for the time you spread that rumour about Stacey and her younger brother.

But you haven't got the money yet.

DON'T PANIC, HOMBRE! We're about to get it sorted.

What follows is a gentle reminder that you already understand money, even if you can't read the middle pages of the *FT* without having a seizure.

Remember simple and easy? Money is both. It really is. It's binary; it's numbers on a screen.

Back in the day, before we could mould salt into tablets, bartering was the norm. That's when you'd say to Fred the barrel-maker, '*Fred, I like your barrels, I reckon one of them is worth about the same as this length of hessian. Swap you.*'

And then money came along and complicated things.

But let's make it simple again.

Cash gets you stuff you need and want. (Need comes first.) Don't be afraid of it.

Think of one of your heroes. Pick somebody well balanced, affable, with empathy and emotional intelligence, and have a look at their attitude to money. It's probably a bit different to yours, no?[52]

Now, try and be like them. Copy what they do. You will soon be sorted.

YES – I know, you know. We all know. Money's not *that* important. But, unfortunately, if you want to implement a lot of the other shit in this book you're going to need a home to go to and food in your stomach and for that you'll need sufficient levels of cash in your account.

---

[52] There are also plenty of very wealthy individuals in the world who are fucking insane. Pick your heroes wisely.

Cash is your passport to collecting essential supplies and non-essential experiences. That sounds like the recipe for happiness! Oh BOY, money is SO COOL!

What a difference it makes to know that you can send Petronella to her donkey-gymnastics class this weekend without having to apply for another credit card!

You have a relationship with money, whether you like it or not and you need to decide NOW who's going to be the boss.

YOU need to be dominant partner; you need to be the top. It's about control. You can either be slave to financial demands, or you can master the money-monster with a steely determination.

So opt for the latter.

Make money your bitch and watch your confidence grow and your bank balance actually *balance*, rather than veer staggeringly in and out of the red.

WORK AND MONEY LESSON 6:
HOW TO MAKE MONEY

YOU'VE MADE THE decision to work for yourself. Good. Because your previous job wasn't safe and there was nothing you could do about it.

You're not scared of money any more. It's just numbers. So now you've got to make some.

How are you going to do that? Not sure? Don't worry. This is how you make money:

Sell stuff for more than you paid for it.

Whatever it is – your time, your barbecue-in-a-box starter kit, your crate of Taiwanese left-footed plimsolls, your body. It doesn't matter.

You sell shit, you get paid.

So work out what you're going to sell.

Perhaps you're going to sell an *object*? Perhaps you've know a dude who knows a dude who's got a brother in Sri Lanka who owns a rubber-glove factory? That's great. People always need rubber gloves. Sell those.

Perhaps you rue the day you ever emigrated back from Italy because nobody does liquorice ice-cream like Giuseppe on the Piazza del Campo. Call Giuseppe, get him to send you a crate-load and flog them to the next-door neighbours.

Or perhaps *products* aren't your bag. Products are difficult to source and you don't know anybody in Pakistan or anybody called Giuseppe.

No worries! You can become a CONSULTANT!

The beauty of consulting is that anybody with an ounce of skill can do it. Choose your niche and EXECUTE.

You know SOMETHING. There's *at least one* single thing that you know enough about to package up and sell. If you're cunning and convincing and committed, you'll be able to identify somebody who wants to know what you know and will pay you for it.

What are you good at? What do people come to you to advice for? That's the kind of stuff that you can charge for.

What about the hours you've spent on online poker when you should have been working? That's left you with some residual cardsharp skills, surely?

Or the time you got your head stuck in an electric fence after a night of cider-drinking and cow-pushing? That left you with a superhuman tolerance for pain and no left ear. The army could find a use for you as a test subject.

Or perhaps you've got advanced knitting skills? Great! Knit something cool, like a beer-mitt, and sell it. Then make a real living by showing people how they can knit their OWN beer mitts. You're halfway to a million already.

BUT! Even if you're really good at, say, koi carp inoculation or have a gift for divining wild truffles or curing cats of their manic depression, all the mad skills in the world are useless if you can't sell them and you can't charge for them.

So go back to the beginning of the book and re-read the chapter on self-confidence.

Fake it until you make it.

Then stop faking it.

Pay particular attention, however, to your chosen niche. It's not smart to attempt surgery or simultaneous interpretation without a solid grounding in the skills needed.

Of all the practical and simple steps in the book, this is the one you won't take. You won't take this step because you're scared. You're scared because you've got responsibilities. You're scared because it might not work out. You're scared because you don't know if your idea is any good or because starting businesses is the domain of those imaginary *other people that exist in your head.*

The difference between *the other people* who start their own businesses and *those who don't* has nothing to do with genes, therapy, opportunity or dental records.

It's down to something you have already learned. It's down to giving yourself permission and having the confidence of a saint at the pearly gates.

You can start your own business and you *should* start your own business. You can do it, because you rock.

WORK AND MONEY LESSON 7:
NOTHING IS FREE

HAVE YOU MADE money your bitch? Good. You'll need to, because NOTHING IS FREE.

Oh great, another blinking platitude from a book that should have been subtitled 'A Collection of Common Sense'.

You know that everything comes at a price, right? You know that there's little – nay, NOTHING – upon this planet that is free? You pay for everything you get, either in advance, slightly later or a long way down the line.

How many times have you been tempted by a gym membership because you got three free carcinoma-friendly sunbed sessions with it? What about the new car that came with a FREE bottle opener and fox-fur drape? And the bank account that gives you 20 quid and a key ring when you open it?

Well guess what? None of that was free. It had a manufacturing cost or a service cost. This cost wasn't borne by the seller. No matter what you are told. You have paid for this.

In the less salubrious side of product sales, there's a technique called bump and drop. This is when you get a discount off an artificially inflated price. The thing is, it isn't *artificially* inflated at all. It's just the price. The price of anything is the price that somebody is willing to pay for it.

How much would you pay for a piece of paper that had been signed by me? Not much, perhaps. So that's how much I will sell it for – not much.

But how much for a piece of paper that has been signed by the spirit of Elvis Presley? You'd pay a lot more. And that's how much it is then worth.

But back to free.

There's monetary-free, there's time-free and there's karma-free.

If your boyfriend buys you a bunch of flowers, it may come with no apparent strings attached. But later on, perhaps much later on, it will be used as a 'get out of jail free' card or a 'blow job' card or a 'night out with the boys' card.

Hell, it might not have been the intention, but it builds up in the favour-bank.

This is the law of reciprocity. If you want somebody to do something for you, give them something first. If you want them to open a bank account with you, offer them a free pencil sharpener. If you want them to buy your fighter jet, hold the sales conference in a Caribbean strip club with magnums of Cristal champagne and Russian girls available for extra services.

Free inside: a piece of plastic tat that your two-year-old will play with for six minutes, almost choke on, then forget forever. That doesn't seem free to me, that seems pretty expensive.

Free for readers: a CD of some guy that was famous about 15 years ago for writing a catchy pop song about umbrellas. It's not free, it's been paid for by somebody. It might be free to you, but you're giving your time in listening to it.

Free use of the sunbeds when you buy a ticket to spend the day by the overpriced pool in the Costa Del Chav. Well, not free actually, just paid for in the price of your ticket.

You buy a lottery ticket for a quid and you win five million? That's free, isn't it? Well, no. It was paid for by the other five million lottery ticket buyers. And it will be paid for by you in kidnap insurance and personal protection and financial advisers and lawyers and security systems and paranoia.

If you expect something for nothing, you'll get bitten.

'But,' you say, 'but I love to do free stuff. It's my charity thing. I do it for the sense of wellbeing that comes from dishing out soup and sandwiches to homeless people.'

Good for you. And I suppose you don't tell anybody about it? And you don't expect to go to heaven as a result?

I'm not knocking you for doing it, quite the opposite. Anybody who spends time looking after other folk is a good person. YOU ARE A GOOD PERSON. But you haven't done something for nothing, you've done something for something.

We all do. It's give and take in equal proportions, even if the currency doesn't look the same.

WORK AND MONEY LESSON 8:
HOW MUCH MONEY YOU NEED

YOU'RE WORKING FOR yourself. You're enjoying a modicum of success. You're not sure when to stop and take that holiday.

You need to work out how much is enough.

If you don't know how much is enough, you'll end up chasing the dollar until you can't run any more and on your deathbed you'll realise that you had all that you wanted years ago.

So, you're going to draw up a list of what you NEED and what you WANT.

Things you need will include food, one good pair of shoes for each member of the family, a change of underwear and the occasional celebratory pint of shandy to mark special occasions.

Things you want might include an adventure playground for your troupe of tame grasshoppers, a collection of tie-dyed pumice stones and an alarm clock that wakes you up with a mild electric shock. (I've always thought this would be an excellent idea as a motivational tool for recalcitrant adolescents.)

By the way, unless you're supporting 36 kids, two avaricious ex-wives, a flotilla of 18th-century schooners and a debilitating cocaine addiction, you don't need millions.

Once you've got that list of stuff that you realistically need, review it. Take out any mention of equine pedicures, cars with Italian-sounding names and subscriptions to *Readers' Wives*.

Done that? Good. Now work out how much all of the stuff on your 'need' list is going to cost you.

Now double it.

You now know how much money you need.

The reason you doubled it is because you forgot about taxes and you forgot about the boiler breaking down each winter despite the expensive annual maintenance. You forgot about stumping up the bail money for your brother Frank and you forgot that the kids are going to come home from school every other week with a sponsorship form.

Save 25 per cent for long-term savings and save another 25 per cent for lump-sum payments for *really* important stuff, like holidays and roof repairs and taxes and kidnap insurance.

Simple.

WORK AND MONEY LESSON 9:

HOW TO HANG ON TO YOUR MONEY

THIS IS ABOUT *want* and *need* as well. It's about growing up and not wasting your pennies on overpriced and unnecessary crap.

I'm not going to repeat the oft-repeated advice about dropping the small pleasures. '*Stop going to Starbucks*', '*brown bag your lunch*', '*make your own clothes from banana skins and plastic bags*'.

You've heard these suggestions before. This isn't advice for saving money; this is advice for avoiding starvation. If you're eschewing a £3 cup of coffee three times a week because you can't afford it, you need to go back to the *making money* bit so that you've got some real cash to save.

Much as knowing when to stop collecting money in return for work or sweat or stress is the key to being happy, knowing when to stop buying shit is the key to holding on to your cash.

You need to tell yourself that ENOUGH IS ENOUGH, but that gets more difficult the more you have.

So this is how you hold on to your money:

There's a ton of shit you could live without, but, as your social circle widens to include folk with titles before their triple-barrelled surnames, you're going to be doing a lot of keeping up.

YOU DON'T HAVE TO KEEP UP.

Spending money is really, really easy. If I gave you a thousand pounds and asked you to spend it, you could do it in less than five minutes. If I gave you 20 thousand you'd have no problem; ditto with 50 or 75 thousand. Spending a couple of million could be done in a matter of days, and any eight- or nine-figure amount might take a few weeks to spend on shit that's actually available to buy, but you'd manage it.

Whatever the amount, spending it takes less time than actually making it.

So – again, as if you actually need to be told this – don't spend money on a load of shit you don't need.

If you see something you like the look of and have to ask yourself if you can afford it, you can't.

LUXURY IS ONLY A LUXURY IF YOU CAN AFFORD IT.

If you can't afford it and have to borrow to book next winter's trip to Aspen, you are fucked.

If you're tempted to buy your pocket poodle a diamond tiara, stop and think. If the private members' club that's only open two weekends a month and only sells magnums of Dom Perignon and buckets of oysters to women with tans and men with long hair, stop and think. That collection of koi carp? You don't need it. Another Arabian stud farm? No.

Buy yourself a bottle of sherry instead.

That's how to save money.

WORK AND MONEY LESSON 10:
TAKE THE PAYMENT PLAN

YOUR CREDIT CARD is not your friend. Your credit card is, rather like work, one of those deviant necessities of life that needs to tolerated, not celebrated.

That's because you've not been taking responsibility for yourself. Credit is never free – nothing is free, remember – and you managed to accumulate debts to the tune of 17 thousand pounds because you couldn't resist the lime-green chaise longue and a collection of 'ironic' Hello Kitty duvet covers.

Up until now you couldn't live without your credit card because you couldn't live without credit. But you couldn't live responsibly *with* your card, could you? Nobody was there to hold your hand, were they? Nobody to say, '*Dude, you really don't need to go out to dinner six nights a week because you're scared of missing out on seeing Jennifer get drunk and take her clothes off. She'll do it again next week.*' Nobody was there to say, '*Do you think you could last a few months without the Live Underwater Poker Channel?'* or *'You know, I'm not convinced that the diamond dentures are a great look.'*

Cut up your card.

Then buy stuff on a payment plan.

'What? What? What?' you say! *'Buy stuff on a payment plan? What ungodly advice is this?'*

Here's the reason:

If you want to replace your ghettoblaster with a new-fangled personal stereo device that you can fit in your pocket and use to play your collection of Celine Dion cassettes, but the personal stereo device costs £100 and you can only afford £22, take the £22-a-month option.

Then, next month, you'll want something else like a ride-on lawnmower or some neon pole-dancing gear or a trip to the greyhound track, but you'll realise you don't have any money because you're spending your spare £22 a month on being able to listen to music WHILE YOU WALK AROUND.

So you don't buy it. You can't put it on your credit card, because that's in the bin, and, hey presto, you aren't going to overload yourself with a ton of crap you don't need.

And yes, the payment plan option is often a little more expensive. But it's magic. You can get hold of lots of nice stuff you can't really afford, without really borrowing.

Brilliant!

WORK AND MONEY LESSON 11:

ACHTUNG! IT'S NOT ABOUT THE MONEY

DUDE, DESPITE EVERYTHING that's come before this bit, it's really NOT ABOUT THE MONEY

You've got this far. You've got your finances well and truly licked. Not a spare cent is going to be dropped on extraneous shit unless you can account for it or justify it by the rule of FUN.

You're working for yourself, so your income doesn't depend on the whims and nonsense of some arsehole boss getting up on the wrong side of bed and taking his chagrin out on you.

You're saving a bit, you're enjoying a lot. Twenty-five per cent of your income goes into your long-term savings, the one that's going to keep you supplied with adult incontinence pads, romance novels and fruitcake in your old age. As a bonus, it's going to pay for Rupert and Amelia to get through school, college and rehab.

You've spent the other 25 per cent on the stuff that keeps you alive and keeps you sane.

Bravo. Well done you. You've come on miles since you opened this book and you're on the verge of your renaissance. But, before you start implementing and earning and saving and being all-star awesome, there's a key element you can't afford to forget:

It's NOT about the money.

You've got a grip on cash and you're reaping it in.

Yeah, well, shit.

You've got your customised Roller and your engraved Rolex and your gated compound with staff to keep your garden green.

Your business partnership is going OK. Your 65 employees like you enough to turn up every day, but your five kids don't always feel quite the same about school. That's the five kids you know about.

You've been married to your first wife twice, your second wife left you for her nail technician and it seems, unfortunately, that the third is an alcoholic. She hides it by going to bed at four in the afternoon. For years you thought she was just sleepy.

Your house is SPOTLESS. You outsource everything to the Filipinas who clean up after you. You don't need as many as you've got. (Four? Five?) The swimming pool doesn't get used much, but the gym looks REALLY COOL, even if it's not very functional.

You did some AWESOME deals last year. You brought in more new business than anybody else in the firm, despite looking after all the other nonsense that has to be done. You don't understand a lot of your whining salespeople. I mean, you can pull in six times the profit they generate and you've got at least three times as much on. Consequently, you're looking at a VERY high six-figure bonus this year. And that explains the hours.

But who cares about the long working hours? The doctor said that the permanent ache in your left shoulder can be remedied with some cortisone injections as soon as you have time. You'll make the time at some stage. In the meantime, you dull the ache with pills.

This year hasn't been good for your arse. Your haemorrhoids have been particularly boisterous, but the rubber-band ligation and endoscopy you had in November nipped those in the butt. The Tramadol were a sweet by-product. You've had a couple of boils lanced as well. You were sitting down too much, apparently.

Sitting down too much? But how does work get done if you're forever swanning around on your feet? It's a desk-bound job and you have to sit at your desk. So plump your derrière down on the chair and GET DOWN TO WORK!

Anyway, the bottom-based discomfort is a small price to pay for a HUGE pay cheque. You get a bit of a hard-on each year at bonus time. You'd never admit it, but as you cash it in you imagine poor people crying. You'd like to fax a copy of your bank statement to the bastards who used to punch you at school. In fact, that's exactly what you'll do. That'll show them.

But money for money's sake is no good, is it? It's what you do with it. And boy, have you got plans. As soon as you have the time, you'll do some really cool shit. You're going to learn to fly a plane one day and charter a submarine. Wouldn't that be cool? And that trip up Annapurna is still on the list of things to do. You reckon three months of training will be necessary before you tackle the ascent – you're not in the best physical shape – but you'll have plenty of time to do that soon. Just a couple more of those juicy bonuses.

Two years, perhaps three. Five at the most, then you can start to take it easy. (Of course, if you get the chance to take the firm public, like you've been aiming for, then five years might be a bit tight. You'd have to stay on in a non-executive position for a little while, perhaps three years more.)

So another eight years tops. In the meantime, you'll get your shoulder seen to and visit your son in the juvenile detention centre – nothing's more important than your health and family.

In eight years (round it off to a decade at the most), you'll have a few million in the bank. In fact, you won't go anywhere until you've got at least 15 million in liquid assets, no point working hard for nothing. By that stage, you'll be able to do anything you want. Really anything. Imagine the freedom. In the meantime, you've got decent childcare for the kids who are still at home. Frankly, they need their mum more than their dad, anyway.

So in 10 years or 15 million, whichever comes first, you sell out and fuck off to the Caribbean and have your first gin and tonic at 11 in the morning.

Bring it on.

Conclusion: The Actual Irrefutable Truth About Money:

It's all a game.

So don't take it too seriously.

If all else fails, remember the 'money can't buy you [insert non-tangible asset here]' adage that's been consoling poor people for years.

Flashing the greenbacks around can get you lots of shit. But it doesn't get you height, wit or good manners.

You can learn one of those. And the other two don't matter.

PART SEVEN

SOME QUICK WINS FOR A WARM FUZZY FEELING

YOU'VE GOT THIS far and now you're ready to implement your new life with gay abandon.

Your foundation's in place. You've dealt with some of the BIG stuff. You've played some serious Jedi mind tricks on yourself. What was once tough is now easy. Where you were once shy, you now enjoy superhuman levels of self-belief. Where you once worried, you now say, 'Fuck it, let's have a beer.'

And you've manned up.

You've got relationships and money and communicating down to a T and you're taking yourself a lot less seriously.

Your final task is to move on to some more quick wins. You've had a few already: you've chucked out the TV, you're going to bed earlier, you're drinking more water.

Here are some more practical steps to take to get you one step closer to awesome and one step further from awful.

These quick wins for a warm fuzzy feeling get you jumping out of bed like a spring-loaded, man-sized flea and racing to the bar for goodness-filled turbo cocktails and nuts.

These quick wins will have you kicking back at the end of the working day with a shit-eating self-satisfied grin on your chops because you've DONE stuff and the stuff you've done makes you feel like a champion.

The beauty of quick wins is that you make progress! Progress is GOOD. Lack of progress equals lack of learning equals lack of evolution equals BAD.

These are a few small but oh-so-vitally crucial steps that you can take to start making the world your own playground.

If you don't change, you will be the same.

THERE IS NO MERIT IN CONSISTENCY.

Do these things and then write me a little note to say how much you appreciated my invaluable advice.

QUICK WIN NUMBER 1:
STOP USING THESE WORDS

REMEMBER HOW YOU need to GIVE YOURSELF PERMISSION to do stuff? This chapter is about that. This is about how you're so tied up in ideas about what's right and wrong; so worried about how the bastions of society will judge you if you don't toe the line that you imprison yourself in other people's ideas.

The words you use are keys to the cell. If you've ever come across NLP[53] during your endless journey through self-help, then you'll understand why WORDS ARE IMPORTANT.

If you don't understand why words are important, take my word for it: words are very important. This is understood by

---

[53] NLP stands for 'Neuro-Linguistic Programming', which is a pseudo-scientific way of saying 'the words we use and hear influence the way we think and act'. If you're interested in finding out more, I'm sure there's somebody out there who can help you.

copywriters, marketing executives and door-to-door salesmen the world over. The words you hear spur you on to action or inaction. The words you USE each day yourself have the same effect. So here are a handful of words you need to drop and the reasons behind your imminent discarding of them.

SHOULD

When you say, 'I should', you likely mean, 'I probably won't.'

- 'I should go to the gym.'
- 'I should stop smoking.'
- 'I should quit reading blogs at work and get on with getting the job done.'

So try this:

For one week, replace 'I should' with 'I will'.

BANG! Watch the results roll in.

'Should' = weak. 'Will' = strong.

Exceptions to the rule:

You should wear your seatbelt, sunscreen, a condom and a crash-helmet in such situations that call for them, even when in doubt.

SHOULDN'T

SHOULDN'T is another nasty little word that propagates stagnation and reinforces the status quo.

Sometimes it's appropriate (you shouldn't kill him, you

shouldn't steal all that money, you shouldn't feed your kids dog-food).

Most of the time, however, it's an update on the Victorian tendency to pander to conformity:

'It's just not done! (Gasp!)'

Some examples:

- You shouldn't wear stripes with checks.
- You shouldn't turn up to a party without a bottle of wine.
- You shouldn't walk on the grass.
- You shouldn't serve gravy without a gravy boat.
- You shouldn't wear jeans to church.
- You shouldn't speak unless you're spoken to.
- You shouldn't question authority.

I CALL BULLSHIT!

So, next time you're faced with a 'shouldn't', ask yourself two questions:

Why shouldn't I?

And what's the worst-case scenario if I do?

The worst case might be better than the current case. You'll find that your life becomes a little easier if you start to jump the fences of social convention.

FREE YOURSELF FROM THE CHAINS!

... and remember, if you do what you've always done, you'll get what you always got.

Exceptions to the rule:

- Men shouldn't wear wigs.
- You shouldn't have sex with blood relatives unless you want really ugly kids and/or to spend the next decade in a secure wing of a maximum-security prison.
- Ladies shouldn't wear tracksuits in public for non-sporting events, unless they are velvety and pastel-coloured.

'WHAT IF'

'What if' can be a useful phrase, when carefully applied. 'What if' can be the beginning of adventure and discovery and scientific invention.

- 'What if the atom isn't non-splittable?'
- 'What if we put some poles on the stage in this gentlemen's club and see what happens?'
- 'What if we dug a well so that we don't have to walk so far for water?'

But mostly, what if is the precursor to a reason for *not* doing something.

- 'What if we get caught?'
- 'What if we get nasty looks from the neighbours?'
- 'What if people don't like it?'
- 'What if it doesn't work?'

What if is a big EXCUSE. Stop using it. It's much easier to apologise than to ask for permission, so drop the 'what if' habit. And while you're at it…

SORRY

Stop saying sorry! Your apology is unnecessary!

If you're one of those people that begin every conversation, phone call or interjection with an excuse – STOP NOW.

There is no need to spend all your days saying sorry all the time, unless you're atoning for genocide[54] or washing whites with colours or something.

- 'I'm sorry to bother you, but do you have…'
- 'Sorry to be a pain, but I was wondering if…'
- 'I hope you don't mind me asking, but…'

You don't need to do this. It says, '*I'm not really very confident at all.*'

ACT AS IF. Re-read the chapter on self-confidence; perhaps you're truly afraid of being a niggling annoyance. Try a bit of exposure therapy. Ask yourself:

---

[54] Genocide: the killing of a large group of people. Not to be confused with uxoricide or avunculicide: the killing, respectively, of your wife or uncle. This footnote isn't really necessary, but I was keen to get those two words into the finished manuscript.

'*What's the worst that can happen if I don't apologise for opening my mouth?*'

I guarantee that you can live with the consequences. Never apologise unless you fucked up. Then apologise once, mean it and move on.

JUST

Just is another way of saying sorry. It takes away the validity of what you're doing. Nobody says, '*I'm just feeding the hungry*' unless they're being sarcastic.

You say, '*I'm just reading a book*' either as an apology or as a roundabout way of saying, '*It's not important and I'll be finished soon. Sure, come round with your holiday photos and ruin my fucking day.*'

So the next time you're asked what you're doing and you're tempted to reply with '*I'm just having a bath. I'll be out in five minutes*', reply instead with, '*I'm having a long, luxurious and entirely self-serving soak in an almond-scented hot tub. See you in a few hours.*'

QUICK WIN NUMBER 2:

WHAT YOU WEAR DOESN'T MATTER

IT DOESN'T MATTER what you wear. It's your choice to dash around in a loincloth or a tutu, if that's how you roll.

Don't let anybody tell you what to wear. Not your wife, not your husband and certainly not your friends.

(Your boss may dictate what you wear, however, if you're looking for a generally quiet life and a pay cheque each month.)

This is because what you wear is of no importance to anybody but you. If you're invited to a black-tie ball, you have the choice of not attending.

Appearance is important, but only so important.

It's important that your clothes are clean. It's important that your clothes are suitable.

But here's the thing. Suitable is currently more or less defined by the spirit of the day by convention, by tradition, by etiquette (yuk!). The *shoulds* and the *shouldn'ts* are at it again.

You decide if what you are wearing is suitable and you pull it off.

There are limits of course. Your boss and the human resources department will have a very clear idea of what is suitable and, as long as you are trading your time for their money, you have an obligation to play their game. If you're playing their game – which you won't be for much longer – you're not making your life any easier by turning up to give a key client presentation in bermuda shorts and a T-shirt that reads 'I Like The Pope, The Pope Smokes Dope'.

Similarly, if you're an undertaker, you'd be ill-advised to wear a white smoking jacket to carry your dead clients down to the crematorium. Not that there's anything *wrong* with it, but there are certain times more appropriate than others to pick your battles and certain people more appropriate than others to battle with. Nightclub bouncers and grieving relatives are never a good choice. They tend to fight dirty.

But otherwise, and coming back to the supposition that you are in an environment where you enjoy the liberty to wear pretty much anything you like, then do just that.

If you want to wear an emerald tiara and a diamante-studded bullet-belt, then wear it. And if your boyfriend wants to wear a T-shirt and jeans to the same event, so be it. It doesn't matter.

Look at the power-brokers. Look at your heroes, your gurus. Does anybody tell them what to wear? No.

So wear what you want[55] and celebrate it.

[55] Except tracksuits, unless involved in some sporting activity or in the comfort of your own home.

QUICK WIN NUMBER 3:

THE MYTH OF 'YOU CAN ACHIEVE ANYTHING'

HEY DUDE! DON'T be down! You're worried that you can't get done what you're thinking of doing? Don't be! You can achieve anything you put your mind to!

Mountaineering? No problem! Within no time you'll be the first woman to ever scale Everest without food or oxygen. Athletics? Hell, yeah! Bring it on! Within six months you'll be running back-to-back marathons and finishing on the leader board each time. You can even solve the Rubik's cube in fewer than 21 moves while blindfolded!

You can give birth to a child genius who will be walking at three months, talking at six months and playing the piano by his first birthday. This same little boy will go on to win an Oscar at 12 for directing the 'Best Foreign Language Film' and by the age of 18 will have a Pulitzer prize AND a Nobel prize for Chemistry on his mantelpiece! You just need to nurture his nascent genius and invest in a bevy of private tutors.

If you study hard enough and apply enough positive mental energy, you'll find a cure for cancer. You'll stop wars and bring love and goodwill to everybody! You want to live to 130? Why not 150? You can achieve ANYTHING!

YOU JUST HAVE TO PUT YOUR MIND TO IT.

Begin the day with positive incantations and watch your excess weight drop off, your wealth increase BEYOND YOUR WILDEST DREAMS and your fertility issues magically solve themselves. Ask the universe for what you need and the universe will deliver!

Each morning, on waking, repeat these mantras:

I am thin and beautiful and rich and fertile and intelligent.

I think, therefore I'm Einstein!

I must, I must, I must increase my bust.

* * *

… and other bullshit.

Or get real.

Even as you approach the end of this book, you can't achieve *anything* and there's no point in trying.

You can probably do a little more now than when you picked up this book. That comes with tweaking your willingness to actually DO stuff, instead of spending hours in front of daytime TV and eating only chocolate, marshmallows and lard pies.

But the idea that you can achieve *anything* is a fallacy. You can't do *anything*. For a start, there's some stuff that is largely forbidden by rule of law or committee[56].

'Rules were made to be broken' is a saying with some merit, but it's not applicable across the board. For example, the signs in city parks that say 'Keep off the Grass' appear to all intelligent people to be an invitation to do exactly the opposite.

If I see a sign that says 'Keep off the Grass', I have to fight the urge to go on a bloody-minded trampling stampede all over the grass while singing, '*Ha ha look at me, I'm on the grass, what are you going to do about it*?' And sure, you CAN walk on the grass if that's what floats your boat. But if you want to live in a city with green grassy spaces instead of muddy brown bogs, acting on your urges to trample on the lawn might be worth reconsidering.

You can also avoid paying your taxes, but compromise is often the wisest course of action when dealing with the taxman, if you don't want to find yourself paying much more heavily down the line.

Other rules make more sense. Rules about being a considerate neighbour, for example, or rules that govern public order, are largely for the common good. You have the freedom to enjoy as much liberty as is compatible with the liberty of your neighbours. You have the right to peace and quiet, and so does your neighbour. If you're playing Def Leppard at ear-bleed

[56] A lot of stuff that's forbidden by rule of law or committee is not forbidden for good reason. A lot of these rules are designed to maintain the status quo and keep the powerful in power. I'm not talking about these rules or laws. I'm talking about the other ones.

volume on a Sunday afternoon, you're not 'exercising your right to freedom'; you're being an arsehole.

And some other rules are hard to disagree with on moral, ethical or pragmatic grounds. You can't, by way of example, have sex with whoever you want to have sex with. You can have sex with whoever wants to have sex with you – and that's in the countries I was raised in – providing they're of sufficient maturity and capable of making that decision unhindered by mental impairment, drink or drugs. Then it's up to both of you – or all three of you – to deal with the consequences.

But even forgetting the rules, the idea that you can do anything is still deeply flawed. There's some other stuff that you'll NEVER be able to do. You already know that you can't *win* a marathon. You missed your chance for that. You can probably participate in a marathon, but putting all your cash on winning would be a waste of money and resources. You're unlikely to be chosen to be mankind's ambassador to the moon. Hello, you're unlikely to ever VISIT space. Statistically, you're not going to write a best-selling children's book or win the lottery.

And on top of the rules and the physical and statistical limitations, there's a whole plethora of stuff that you're just plain NOT MEANT TO DO.

Only you can tell if you're doing what you're MEANT to be doing. And it's not always obvious. Get in the habit of asking yourself at each juncture if your current course of action is worthwhile.

Are you recreating the Palace of Versailles using just toenail clippings and glue? Good for you. You alone can decide if that's right for you at the minute. It could be right for a number of reasons. (Primarily, I would imagine, self-satisfaction.) It won't be right for most people, though, and those people, although they *might* be perfectly able and competent and endowed with a large enough collection of toenail clippings to make it viable, will say, 'Yep, could do, probably, but not for me.'

Similarly, you might decide that decoding the atomic structure of thought is something that you're qualified to do, given your lifetime devoted to molecular philosophy. You're capable of doing it, and you decide that it's worthwhile. I, meanwhile, along with everybody else, will decide that not only can we NOT come close to achieving that kind of result within the few years we have left, but it would also be an utter waste of time to even try.

So you can't achieve anything you set your mind to. But you can DO a lot of stuff.

Instead of focusing on the achievements, focus on the experience. Life is not about how far you swam or how many of your college friends you managed to fit into a Mini Cooper after 18 pints and a pub quiz. Life is not about how fast you unicycled from John O'Groats to Land's End.

Life is about the fact that you swam at all, that you and your buddies tried to fit far too many of you into a small car when drunk and that you even learned to unicycle.

You can't achieve anything you put your mind to. But you can have a lot of fun trying.

QUICK WIN NUMBER 4:
READ A BOOK

WHEN YOU WERE younger, your fear of death by danger didn't exist. You'd swim naked at night in unfamiliar locations, have unprotected sex with people you didn't know, drink with enthusiasm and a lack of regard for public morals, and experience hangovers that didn't take three days to subside.

This was down to inexperience, lack of real responsibility and an irrepressible urge for fun.

But there was something else; something much more important than not being afraid to look like a dick or drink yourself silly in order to boast about it.

When you were younger, you enjoyed a more fertile imagination, stronger beliefs and more dreamy ideals. Now, you've lost the idealism of youth and you're in mourning.

Do you remember how angry you were when you marched on Parliament Square, banner in hand, chanting slogans about child-killers in government? Do you remember how viscerally you defended the rights of beleaguered women in sub-Saharan Africa? Do you remember when you didn't pick your battles because your battles found you and you couldn't turn them down?

Here's why you felt like that:

You used to read more.

You found more hours in the day to exercise your little grey cells. The networks of neurons that ping each other and keep your brain alive were given a thorough workout several times a week.

You could lose yourself in a book for a whole afternoon. You read so avidly that you'd be up until three o'clock in the morning, turning pages, telling yourself, '*Just one more chapter*', until it was seven o'clock and time to go to school.

Now you're older and flabbier, you've got less time for reading.

'*I've got other priorities, for Christ's sake. Read a book? Don't make me laugh.*'

'*The kids need picking up from school. I've got to finish that PowerPoint presentation and the cat isn't going to wash itself.*'

It seems a lot of things have become more important than your 'you time' and you're suffering for it. Your imagination is less fertile. Your beliefs are less important to you and you gave up your ideals with your first mortgage repayment.

BUT IF YOU START READING AGAIN YOU CAN START TO REMEDY THIS.

Here is specifically how to read more and enjoy the benefits of being a more relaxed, informed, intelligent and creative you:

1. Chunk down. Pick up a small book and read 20 pages. Don't do anything else. Don't answer the phone, don't do the washing up. Sit, quietly, on your own. You can be on the bus or in the toilet at work or even at home with your study door closed.
2. Don't give yourself a time limit. If you read 20 pages and don't want to read any more, stop. If you want to continue, carry on. Thirty pages good, forty pages better.
3. Repeat every day for a week. If the book's any good, and you've done more than 20 pages in a stretch, you might just have finished it.

BOOM!
Well done. Now read the rest of *this* book.

QUICK WIN NUMBER 5:
GET RID OF SOME STUFF

YOU HAVE TOO much stuff. You realise this because you know what's important and you know that enough is enough and you know that you've got too much. So here's what you need to do:

1. Get a big bag.
2. Open your wardrobe. Pick out one item of clothing that you haven't worn for 12 months. Put it in the bag.
3. Go to kitchen. Identify something – an apple-corer, a juice-maker, one of your six corkscrews, a chipped plate, a teapot, a pie-dish. If you haven't used it in 12 months, put it in the bag. Just one thing.
4. Do the same with your shoes.
5. Do the same with your books, only this time pick a book

you just know you're not going to read or have read and it was rubbish[57].

6. One other thing – look under the stairs, look in the utility cupboard. Do you have a 'junk room'? Look there.

7. You now have five things in the bag. An accumulation of stuff you don't need that is taking up space in your house. Dust collectors.

8. Now, repeat steps 2 to 6 and get that bag out of the house. Do whatever you want – dump it on a friend, throw it away, give it to charity. DON'T put it in your car to 'deal with later'. GET THE BAG OUT OF THE HOUSE.

BANG!

You now own less. You're getting the upper hand on your possessions.

You rock.

---

[57] This book is exempt from this particular exercise.

QUICK WIN NUMBER 6:
TAKE THE BUS

SICK OF YOUR colleagues? Find your friends TIRESOME and PEDANTIC? FED UP with the perpetual same-old same-old carousel of life?

Yes?

TAKE THE BUS!

By jumping on public transport instead of motoring yourself around in your battered Oldsmobile, you will:

- Meet new people!
- Bolster your immune system!
- Improve your energy levels!
- See more stuff!
- Learn new things!

Does your day look like this?

Troubled sleep – shower to shake the mind-shit from your brain – Smarm FM radio in the car – snarly boss – loathsome colleagues – brown bag lunch – afternoon peppered with ennui – slow, solitary drive home – TV dinner – repeat ad nauseum…

Yes?

Then take IMMEDIATE ACTION!

Starting tomorrow, leave the car at home and jump on public transport. Whether it's the bus, tram, train or subway, the rules still apply and you'll join a tribe of people just like you!

You'll be able to:

- Read more!
- Safely send text messages to loved ones!
- Shut your eyes!
- Get drunk in the afternoon and not worry about having to drive home!

Take the bus and live longer!

QUICK WIN NUMBER 7:
SORT OUT YOUR HOUSE

YOUR HOME LOOKS like shit.

But who cares, right? You rock. And besides, you're never home. You're out shinning up the corporate ladder, slugging scotch with your boss and schmoozing. Who cares that you can't find the light-bulbs?

And when you're knocking about in the back yard, revving your chainsaw and swigging beers with your just-scuffed-enough Timberlands, clean sheets are just an afterthought.

There's a pretty cool installation of empty bottles and pizza boxes in your sitting room, a burn mark where your rug used to be and an array of fungal flora in the bathroom.

YUK.

Frankly, amigo, your place sucks.

You say:

'I'm just not good with that stuff and I don't know where to start. I spend all my money on video games and Coors Light and, anyway, IT'S JUST NOT IMPORTANT.'

But really:

If you ever want to get laid, it IS important.

So, singletons, here's how to get your place looking ready to entertain.

If you can apply the Eight Minute Rule, you've got the makings of a presentable space:

- Pick up your socks.
- If the towel is wet, it does not belong on the floor.
- If it's empty, it does not belong in the fridge.
- If it's no longer edible, it does not belong in the fridge.
- It it's broken, it needs changing.
- If it's wrinkled, it needs ironing.

Once you've got those little tasks sorted, move on to the bigger stuff:

- Paint your walls. You don't have to choose aqua-magento or lime-canary. You don't even need something your landlord would approve, but wet plaster and nicotine stains is not a good look.
- Rearrange your furniture. You don't need to hide your movie collection or move your triple-ply, 80-inch plasma

screen to the spare room. But give your friends somewhere to sit. The floor is not an option.

- Buy some curtains. Cheap ones are fine, but bed-sheets and towels weren't designed to be hung over windows.
- Most importantly, if you have stuff you haven't looked at in a month, used in three, or even touched in 12, get rid of it. This isn't rocket science. Refer back to Quick Win Number 5 and get rid of your crap.

You're smart and creative and capable. And you deserve a home that reflects that.

It's EASY. Do it.

QUICK WIN NUMBER 8:

TURN OFF YOUR MOBILE PHONE AT WEEKENDS

IN THE WAR of man against machine, man is LOSING, but you, dear reader, are winning. Your TV is in the garden and your computer is no longer a limb, but now just an accessory.

But there's one more thing: your mobile phone. Your mobile phone is a bite-sized block of voodoo skulduggery that sits in your pocket, disturbs your sleep and keeps you chained to work, canvassing insurance salesmen and relatives that 'just want to chat'.

'*Yadda yadda yadda, I am SO in control of my life,*' you say. But you're not. You're not in control of who has access to you and when, because you're a SLAVE to that little polished piece of silicon and microchip that sits in your pocket.

Your phone does a lot more than just ring when somebody wants to talk to you. It beeps when you get a message, it hums when somebody tweets you, it buzzes when you get an email, it takes photos, it detects gas, it gives you a back rub when you're tired and fixes you a Bloody Mary when you've got a sore head.

And because of this, you can't live without it, right?

Wrong.

(If you're skimming, read this next bit:)

TURN OFF YOUR MOBILE PHONE.

Here's why: before switching your phone off, this is your weekend:

Wake up to the beauties of the dawn chorus, sense that last night's mutton curry and bottle of Pinot Grigio have been well digested. You've got a clear head and a sneaking suspicion that today's going to be a GREAT day. You pull back the curtains, and you were right. It's a BEAUTIFUL day. You summon the troops from their slumber through the medium of song, eat a breakfast of goji berries and macrobiotic muesli and put on your best khaki bermuda shorts. You're off to the park.

Everybody's dressed, everybody's excited. The frisbee's packed and you've even made cucumber sandwiches like some paragon of English eccentricity. You grab your BlackBerry on the way out, see it's flashing red, and quickly check to see if there's anything important.

WHOA! BAD IDEA!

Alongside various reports from accounting, a rant from a dissatisfied client and suggestions on how to extend your penis from somebody in China, there's a long dirty missive from your boss about your Monday morning deadline. He's NOT HAPPY AT ALL (IN FULL CAPS) about the proposal you submitted on Friday afternoon. *You've FUCKED IT ALL UP AND IF WE SUBMIT THIS PITCH ON MONDAY WE MIGHT AS WELL NOT BOTHER AT ALL.* He wants you to rewrite it in its entirety and he needs to see a draft copy by Sunday morning or your balls are butter.

You sigh. You explain to the family what has happened.

You send the (now crying) kids to the park with their mum, who is threatening to not speak to you all weekend. You spend the rest of the day at your computer, sweating and dribbling and aggravating your carpal tunnel syndrome to make sure the boss is happy. Your boss, incidentally, is on the golf course, not thinking about you even for a minute.

But you can't get any work done because your wife is sending you text messages about every 20 minutes. It's distracting. They say things like, 'I can't believe I married such a spineless loser', 'I should have married Steve, like my mother said' and 'Do you even want us to come home this evening or are you too busy to see us?'

Evening comes quickly and you've achieved nothing, other than developing an acute sense of existentialist malaise. The kids and wife are now in bed. Your wife's text messages have now been replaced with absolute silence that will continue until Monday morning. You sigh for the 18th time today, stick a frozen pizza in the oven and crack open a beer. Just as you sit down to eat, your mother calls 'for a chat'. By the time she finishes telling you about your father's haemorrhoids, Ethel's chilblains and Arthur's lumbago, your pizza is cold and your beer is warm. You get drunk on your own and wake up three hours later in the foetal position, crying.

On Sunday your wife takes the kids to her mother's. You're not invited. You are unable to function due to a crippling hangover and a rapidly draining will to live.

Contrast that with this AWESOME weekend, during which your mobile phone was switched off and hidden in the knicker drawer:

You wake up on Saturday to the beauties of the dawn chorus. The birds are singing solely to you, and they're saying, 'Ooh yeah, Johnny, today's going to be FUCKING-A!' You sense that last night's mutton curry and bottle of Pinot Grigio have been well digested and your morning ablutions confirm it. You manage to shit before you shower – always a sign of good things to come – and you wake up the kids with cuddles and questions about Transformers.

Your wife, who's wearing a diaphanous negligée, makes you eggs Benedict for breakfast, with a litre of weak filter coffee and hash browns on the side.

You grab your favourite khaki bermudas that make you little like Ken off Ken and Barbie, positively don't even think about touching your mobile phone and head off to the park.

The park is full of 19-year-olds in bikinis and, as your wife snoozes lazily beside you, you ogle secretly and innocently.

You play three rounds of mini-golf, have a dinner of stout and oysters and go home. The kids are barely asleep before you and the missus are at it like hammer and tongs on the kitchen table.

On Sunday, you do exactly the same.

Now doesn't that sound like a better weekend?

(By the way, on Monday, you get into the office and your boss apologises for his angry email, but he'd just had a fight with his secretary and wanted to take it out on somebody. Your proposal was just fine.)

Convinced yet? Or am I still hearing objections?

Ah yes, I hear a little objection:

'*If I want to really enjoy my weekend, I need to be able to get in touch with my friends and they need to be able to get in touch with me, right? After all, what if I can't find parking and I'm running late for lunch at Comme Chez Soi? That's why I need my phone, right?*'

WRONG.

Remember 10 years ago, before anybody had a mobile phone? Remember how you used to have fun and meet friends for lunch and get stuff done? Well:

IT'S STILL POSSIBLE.

If anything, we were more organised and more efficient when last-minute changes of plan and calls for information weren't possible.

So, you action plan is simple, EASY and not drastic:

This weekend, switch off your mobile phone entirely. Just try it. You might like it.

CONCLUSION

AS I PUT the finishing touches to this book, I realise that I could keep writing it for a long time.

The rules of getting a grip are simple, but they're not being applied.

Each day, on every street, I see folk angry and upset that the person in front is walking too slowly. I see couples arguing about the behaviour of their friends. I see people worrying about whether their shoes match their belts or whether the conversation they had with their boss this morning is going to cause them misery for the next six months.

I see people suffering from road rage and crying over the fact that their steak hasn't been cooked properly. People are in a rush. People aren't talking to each other. People are taking themselves too seriously.

There's a whole host of shit in life that you have no control over. You can't take responsibility for the stuff that you can't control, so don't. Let it be.

Focus on taking responsibility for yourself and let the rest go. You've got a grip.

~~You rock.~~

NOW MAKE A LIST!

1 — 3 — 5 EVERYDAY.